[SOME QUIRKY PICTURES FROM]
THE NATIONAL WESTERN STOCK SHOW

I0494587

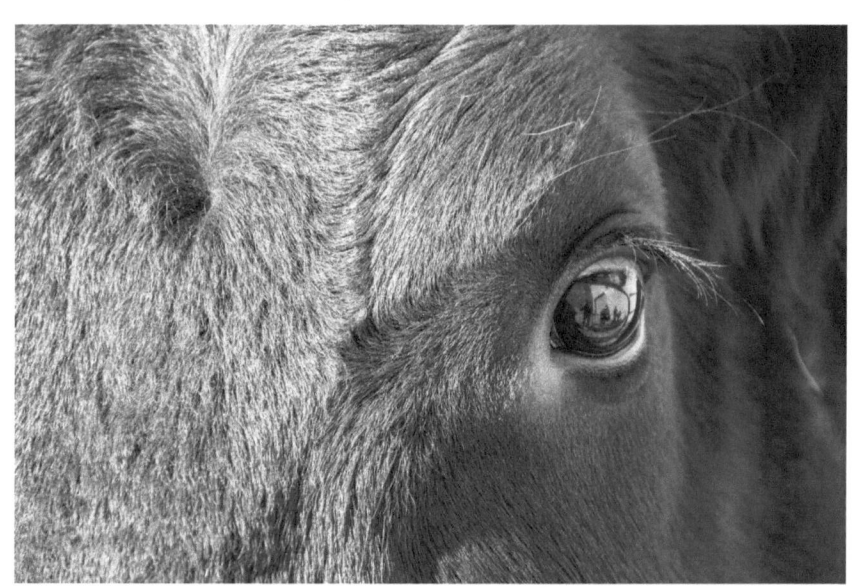

LYLE ROSBOTHAM

As the badge below shows, there have been 110 National Western Stock Shows. I have only attended the last eight. But from my first I realized I was witnessing a part of Colorado culture and tradition that was otherwise invisible to me.

For two weeks every January, the Denver stockyards become a world unto themselves. For the price of admission you get to wander in every obscure corner of that world: hundreds of industrial-strength blow dryers, haircare products for cattle, shower stalls for draft horses. What can be seen backstage is at least as intriguing as what goes on in the arenas.

What started for me as snapshots has evolved into an effort to capture some of the unique flavor and quirkiness of the Stock Show. And now I am hooked: already looking forward to the 111th National Western.

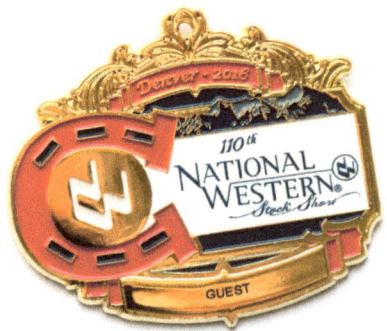

© 2016 Lyle Rosbotham
ISBN 978-0-917796-05-0

Press Four Fifty One
Boulder, Colorado
SAN: 262-0707
www.lylerosbotham.com

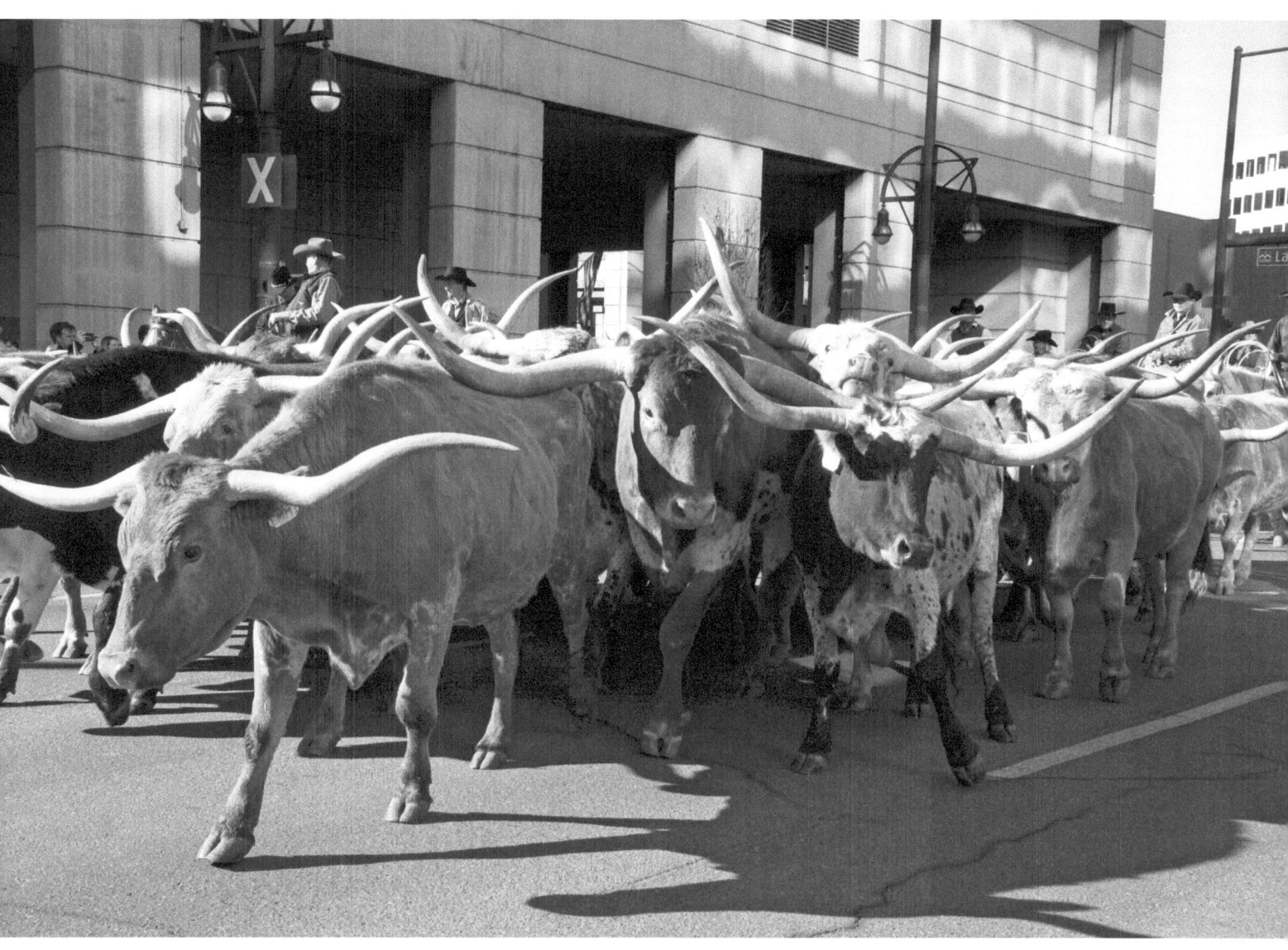

Each year, Texas Longhorns get herded up 17th Street in Denver to mark the beginning of the show.

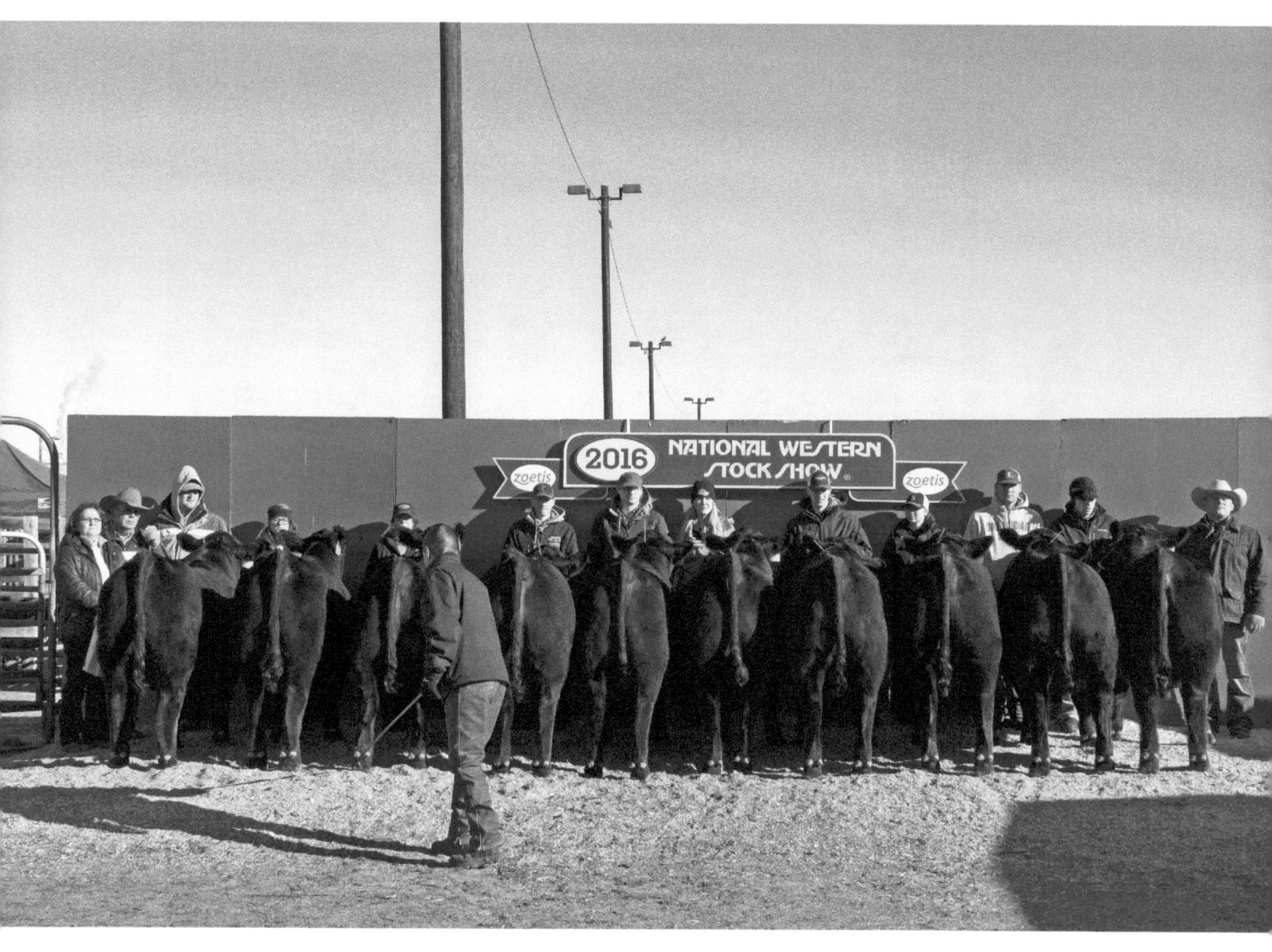

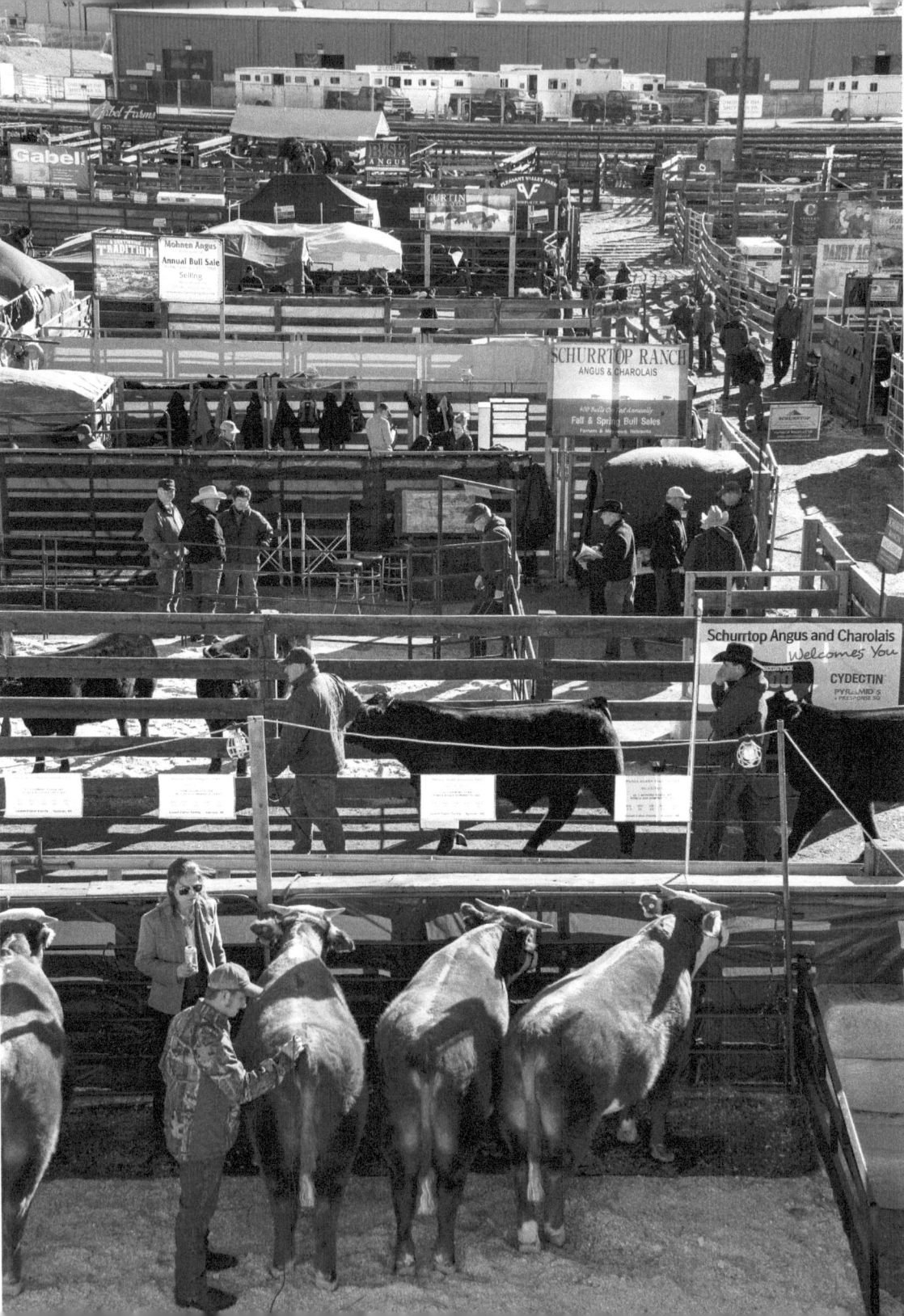

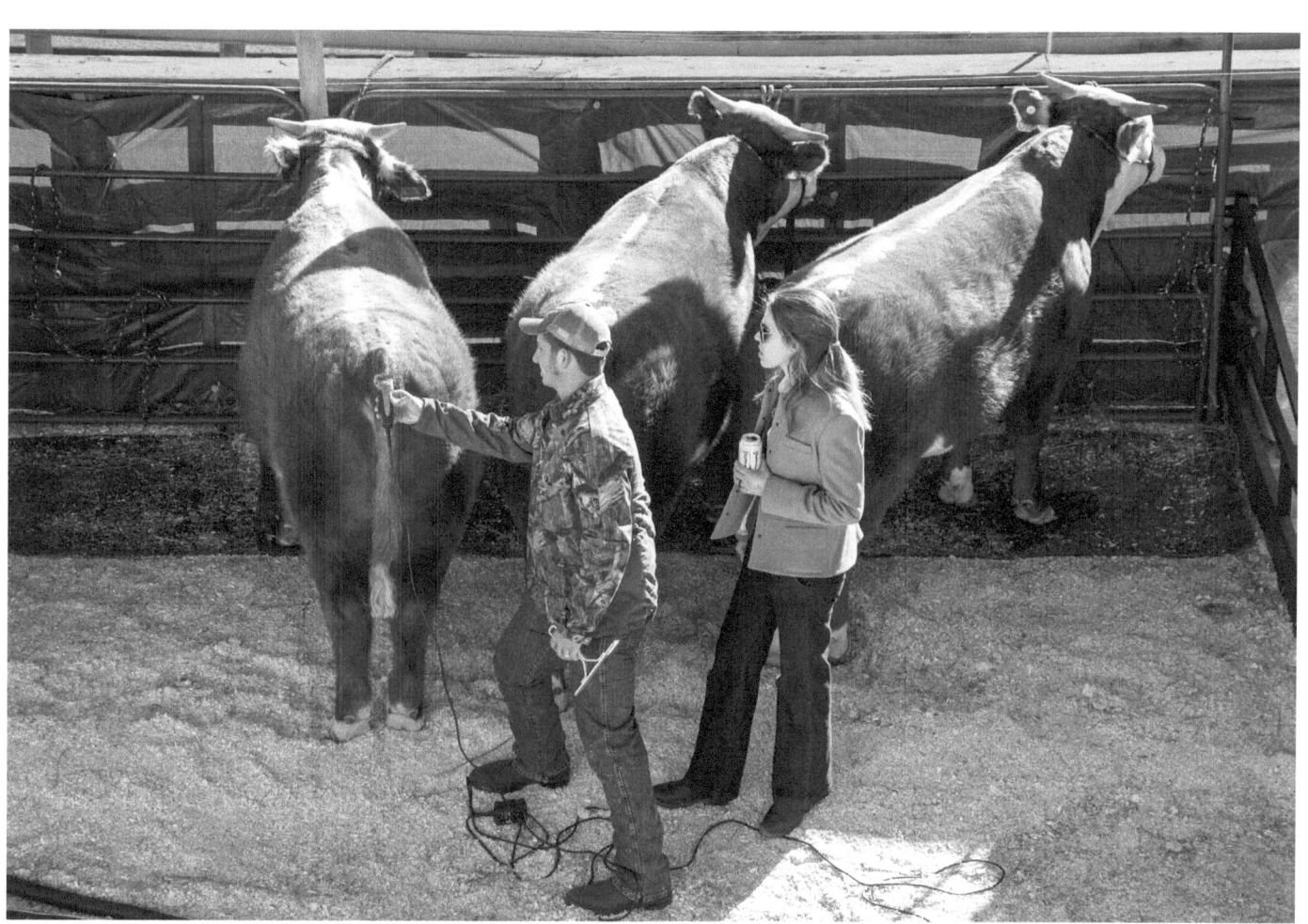

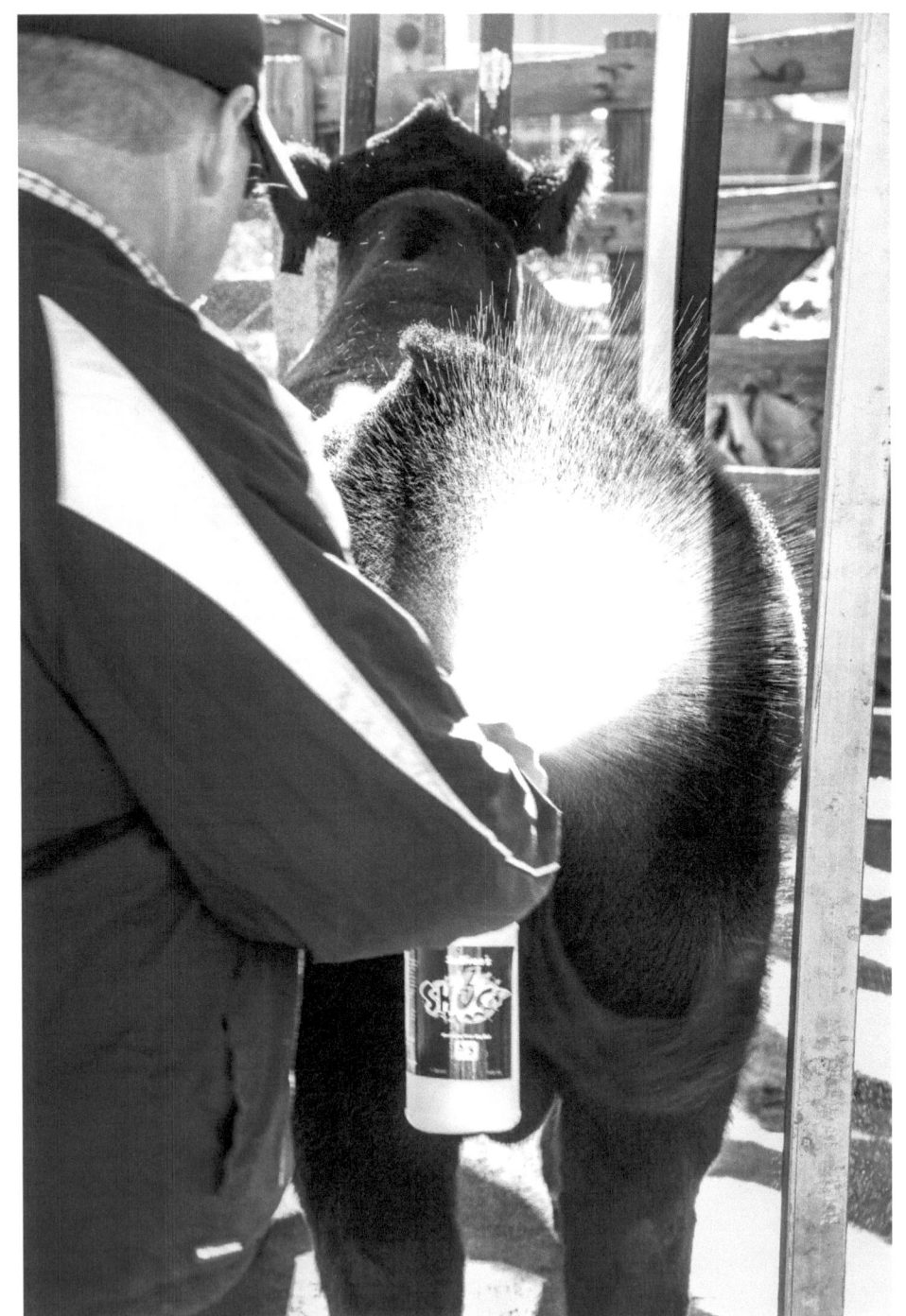

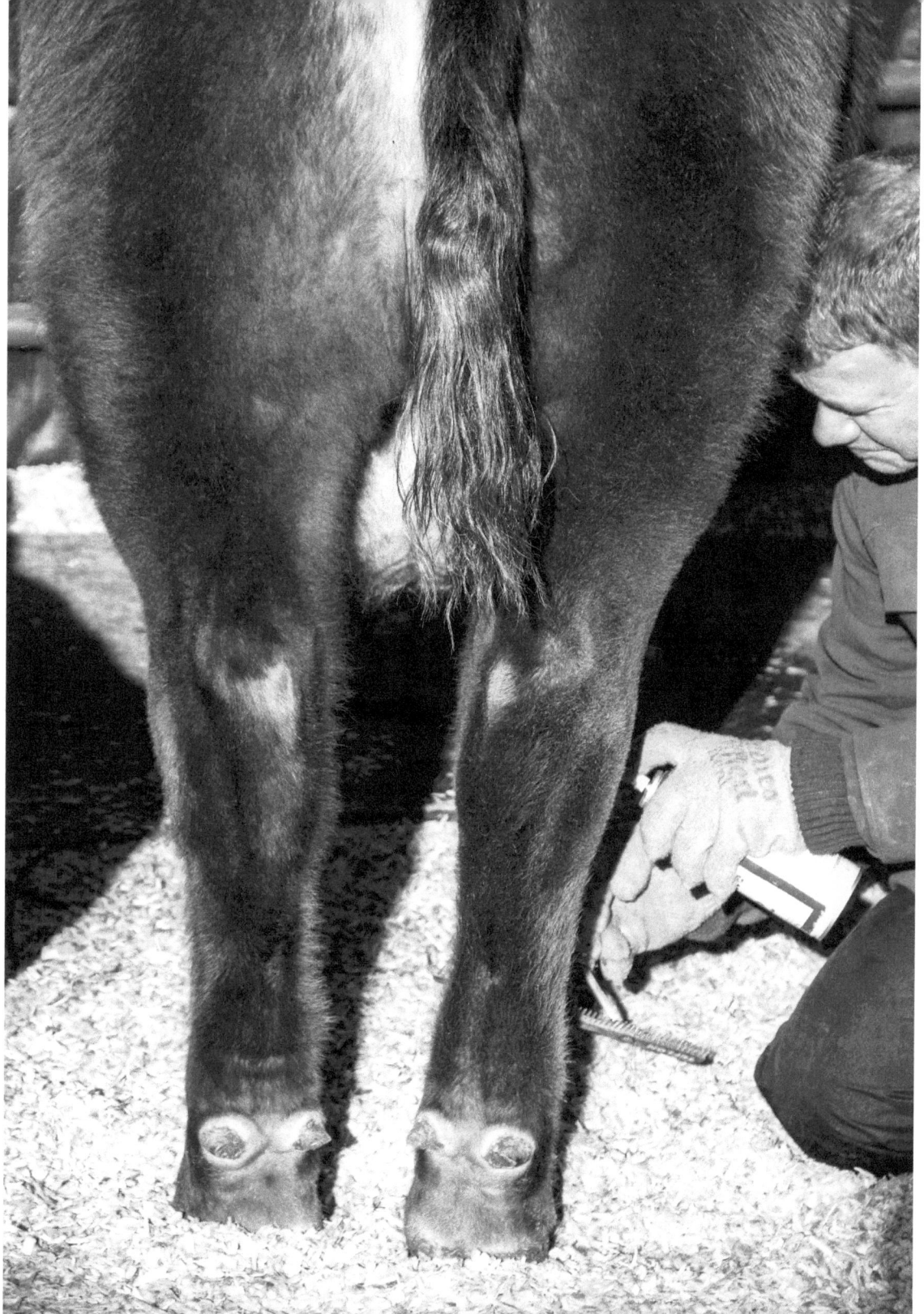

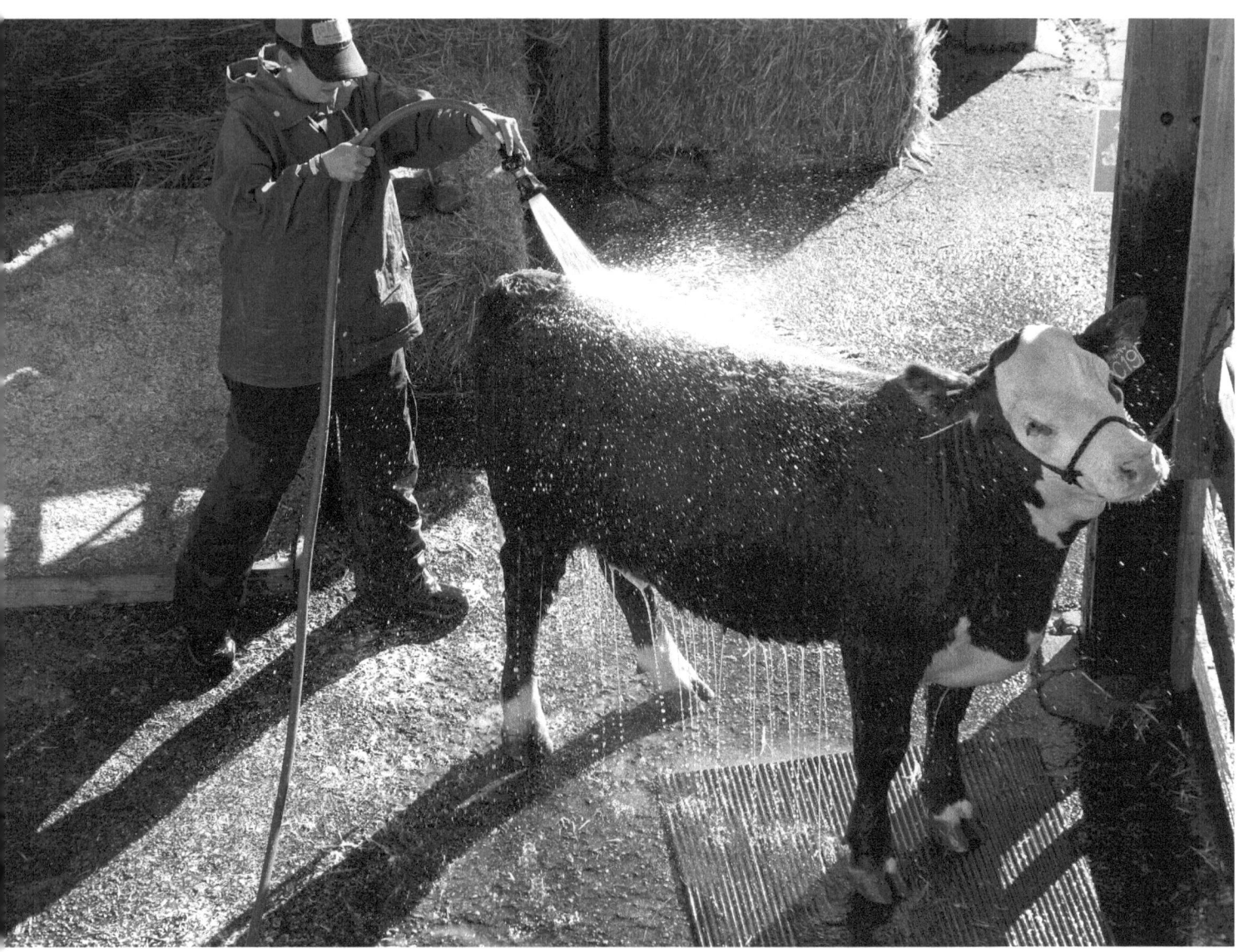

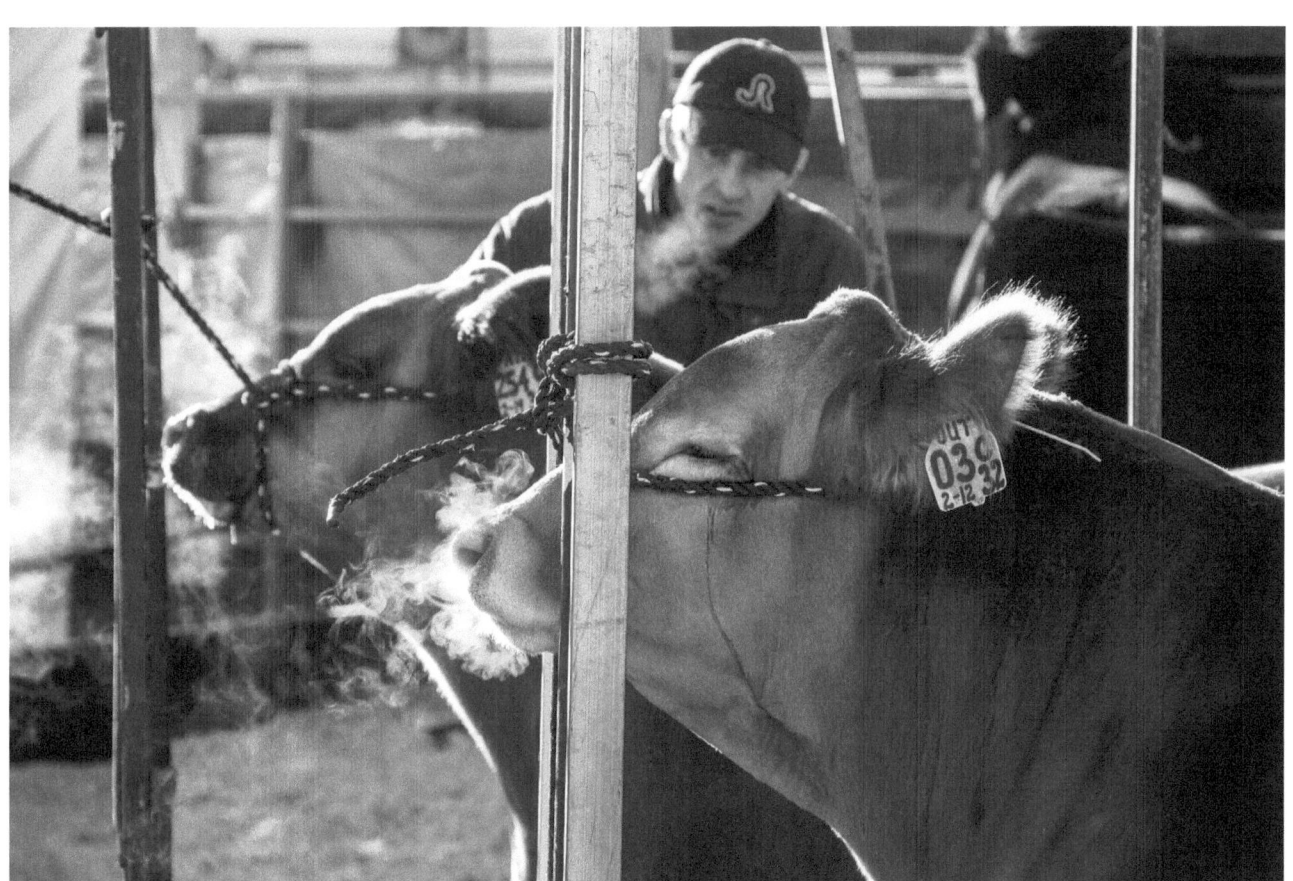

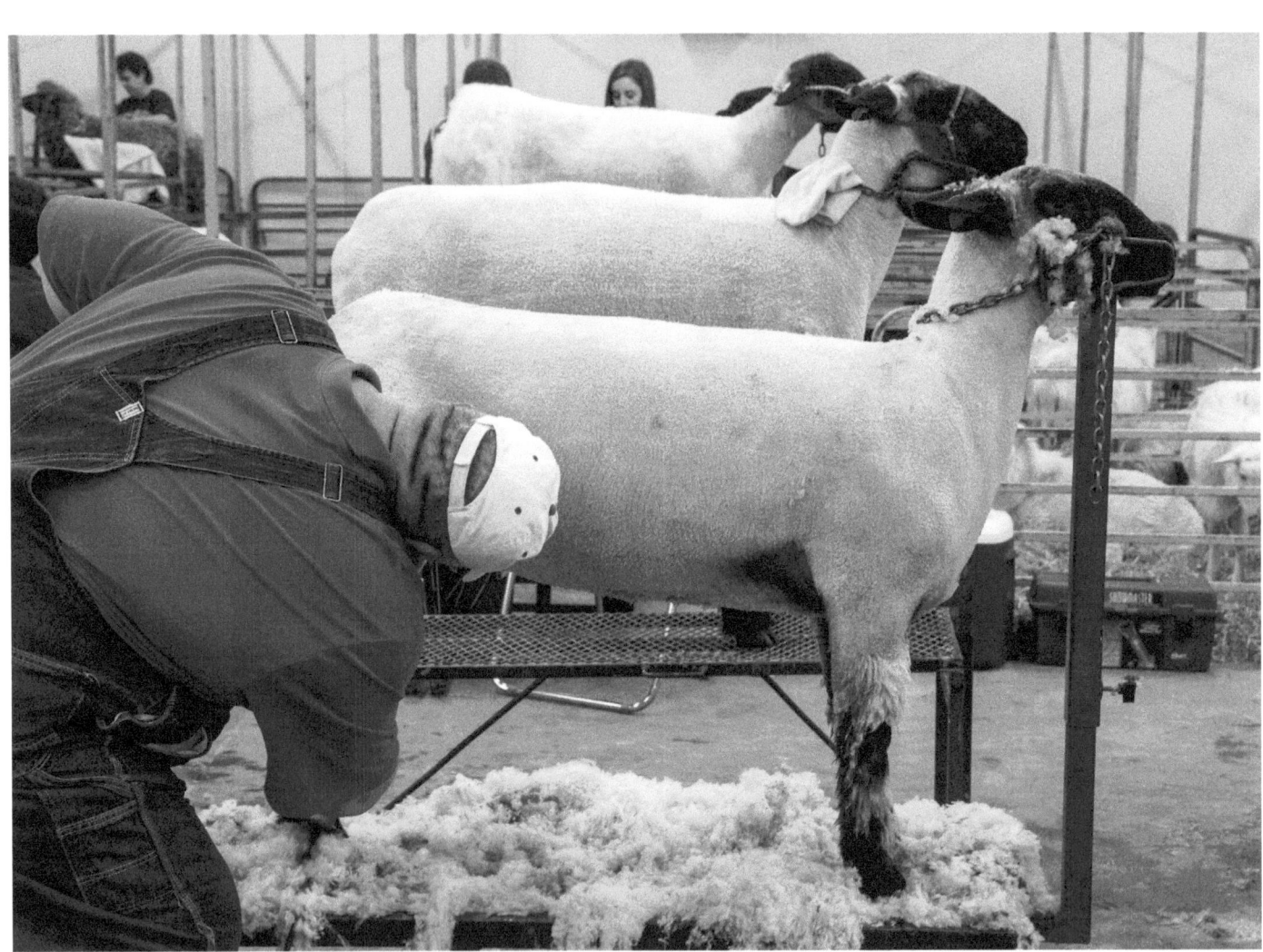

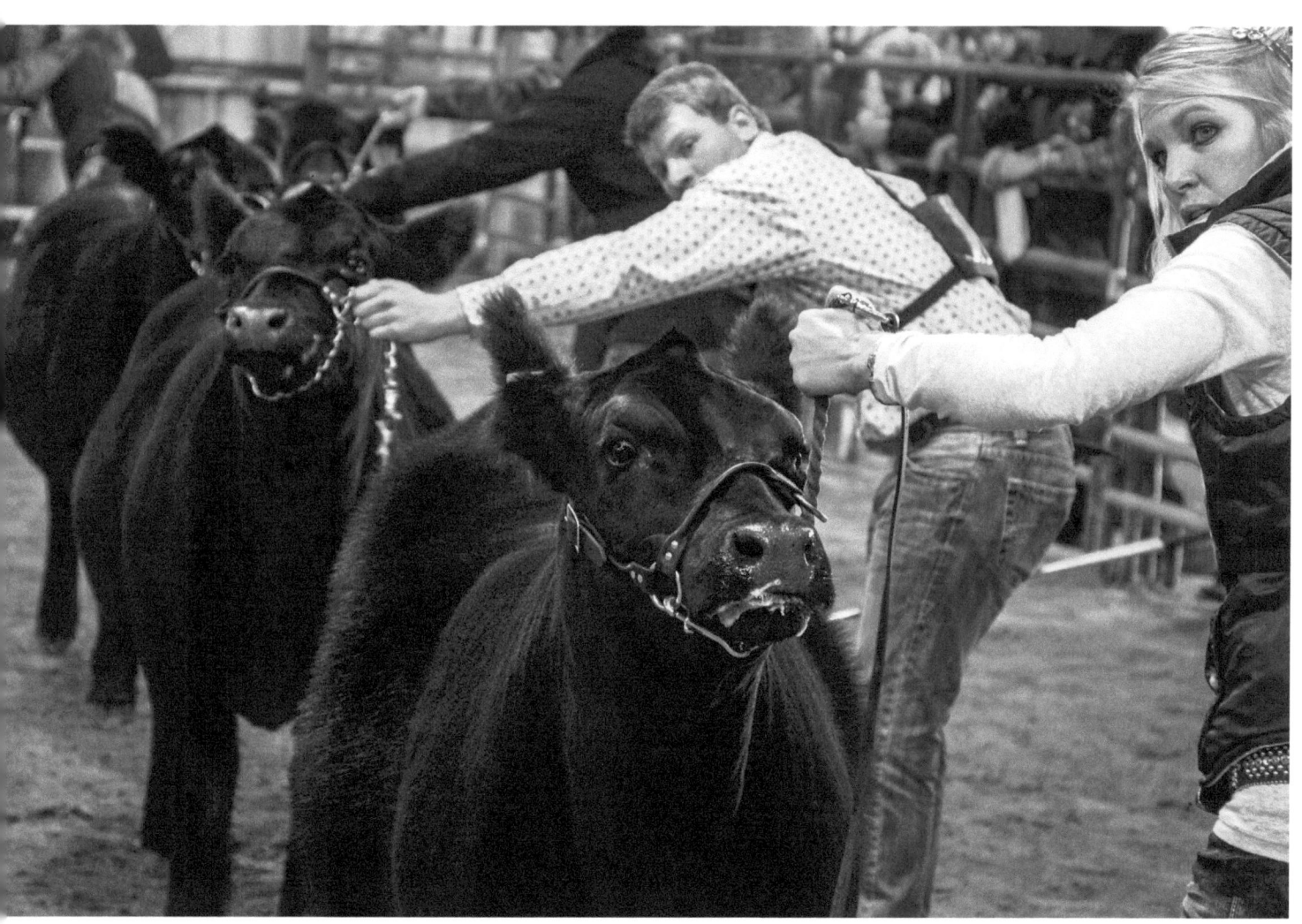

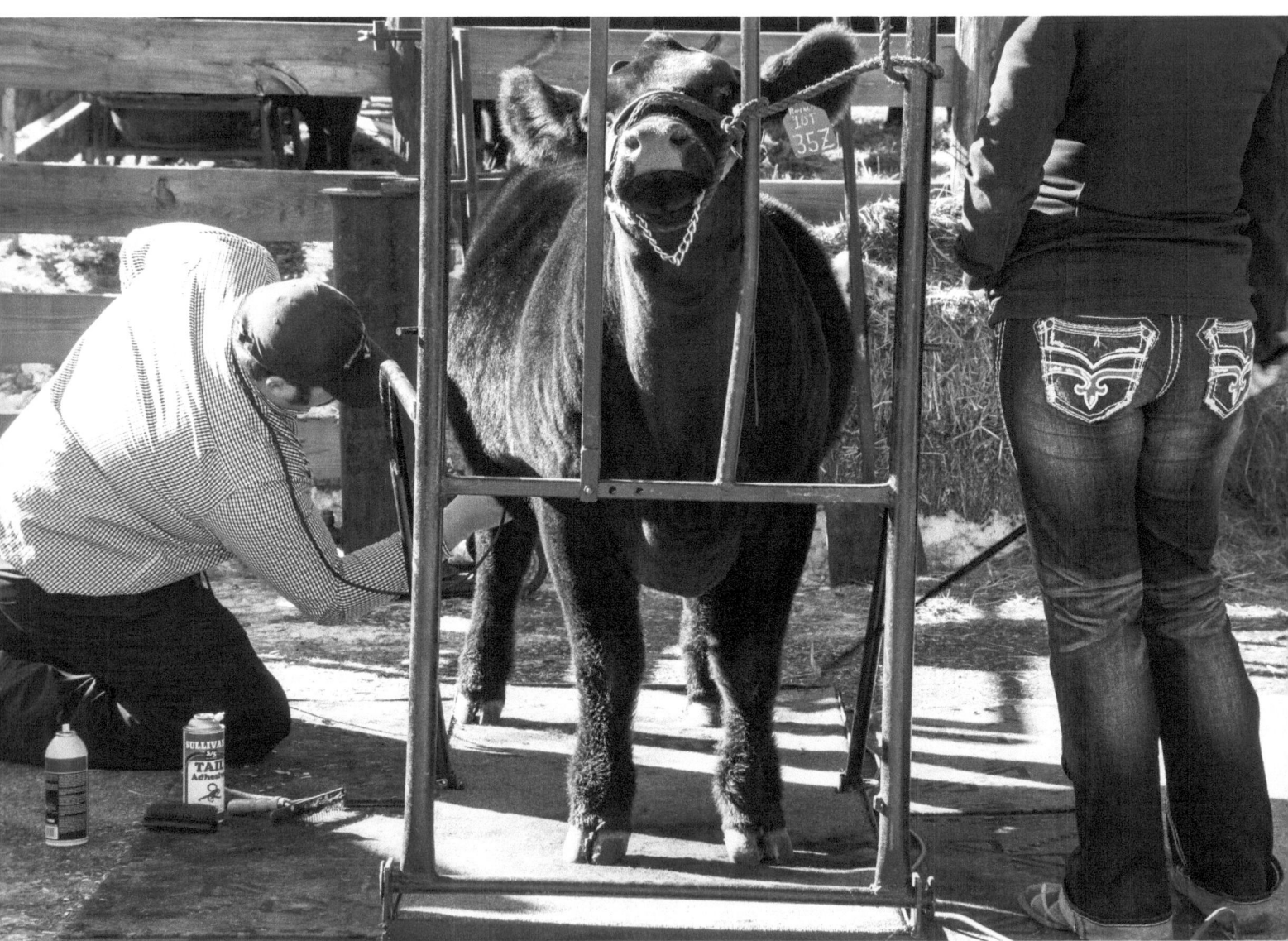

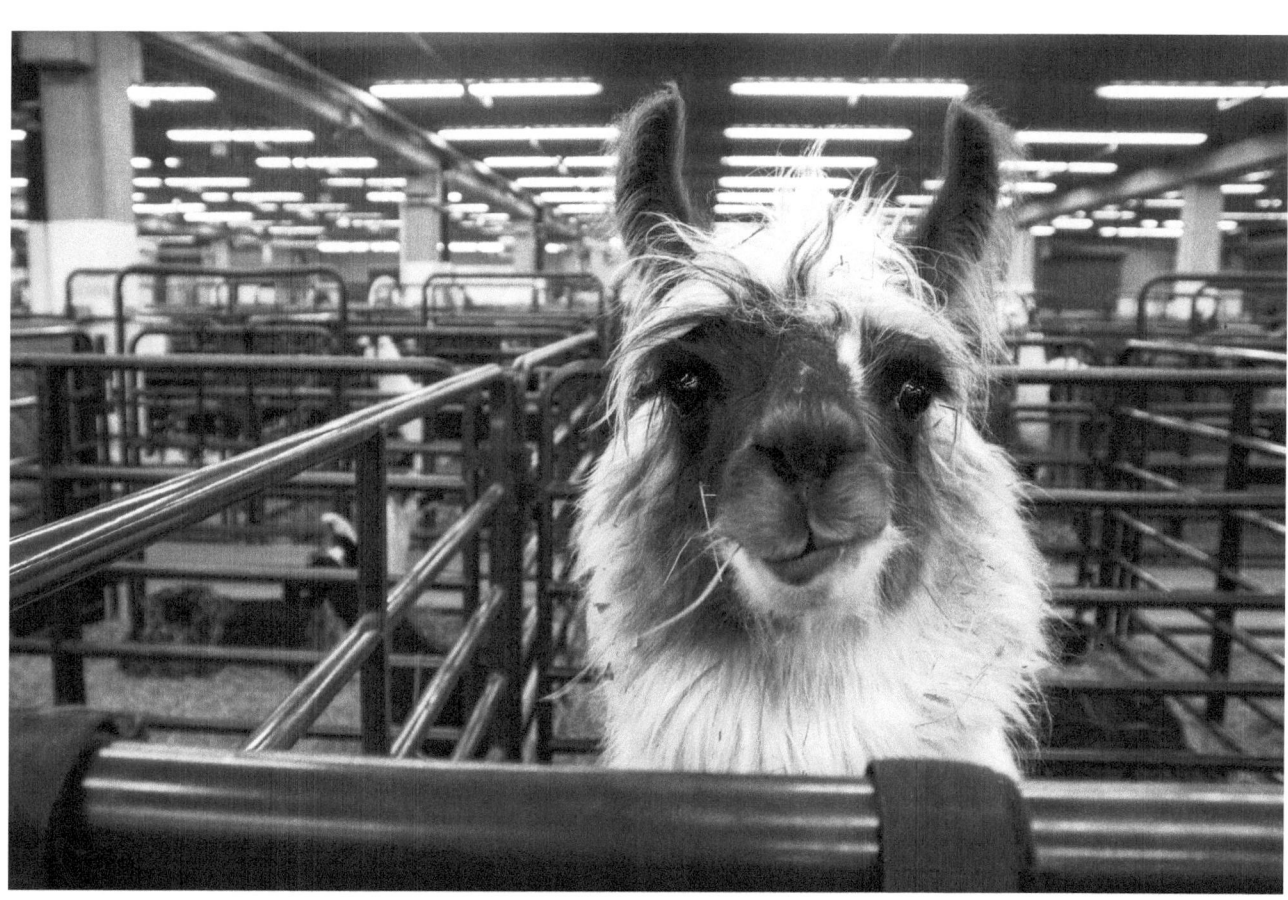

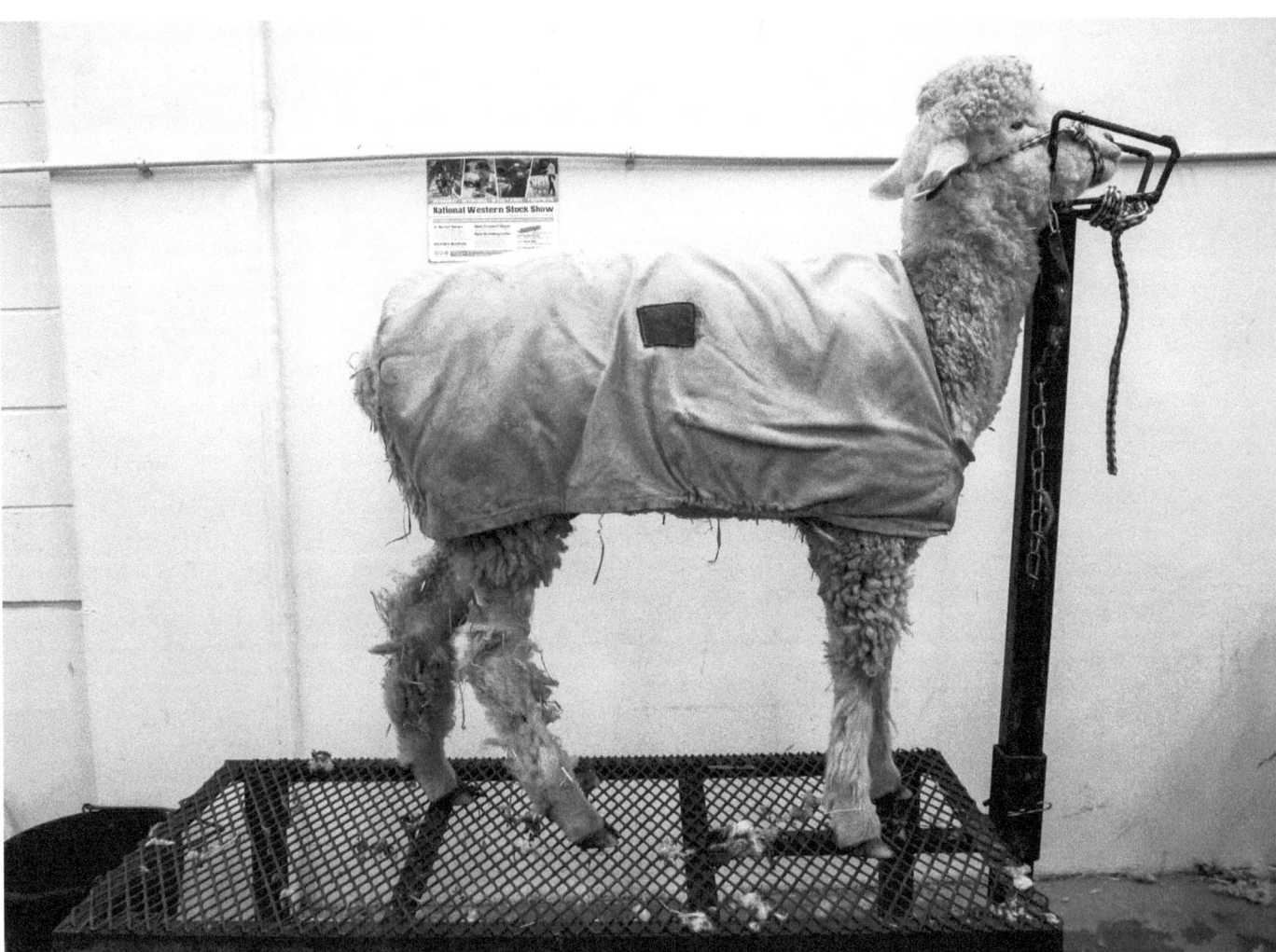

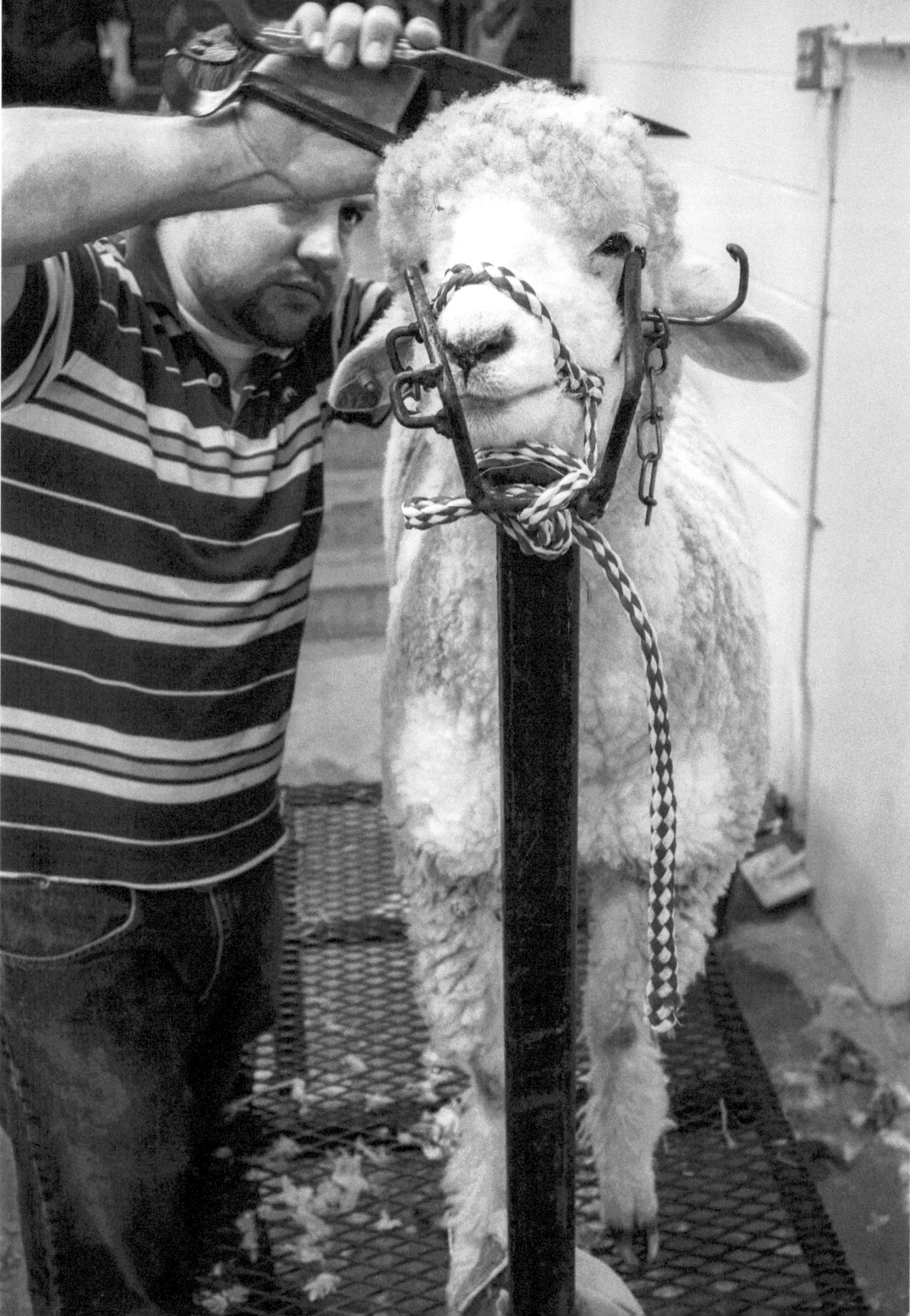

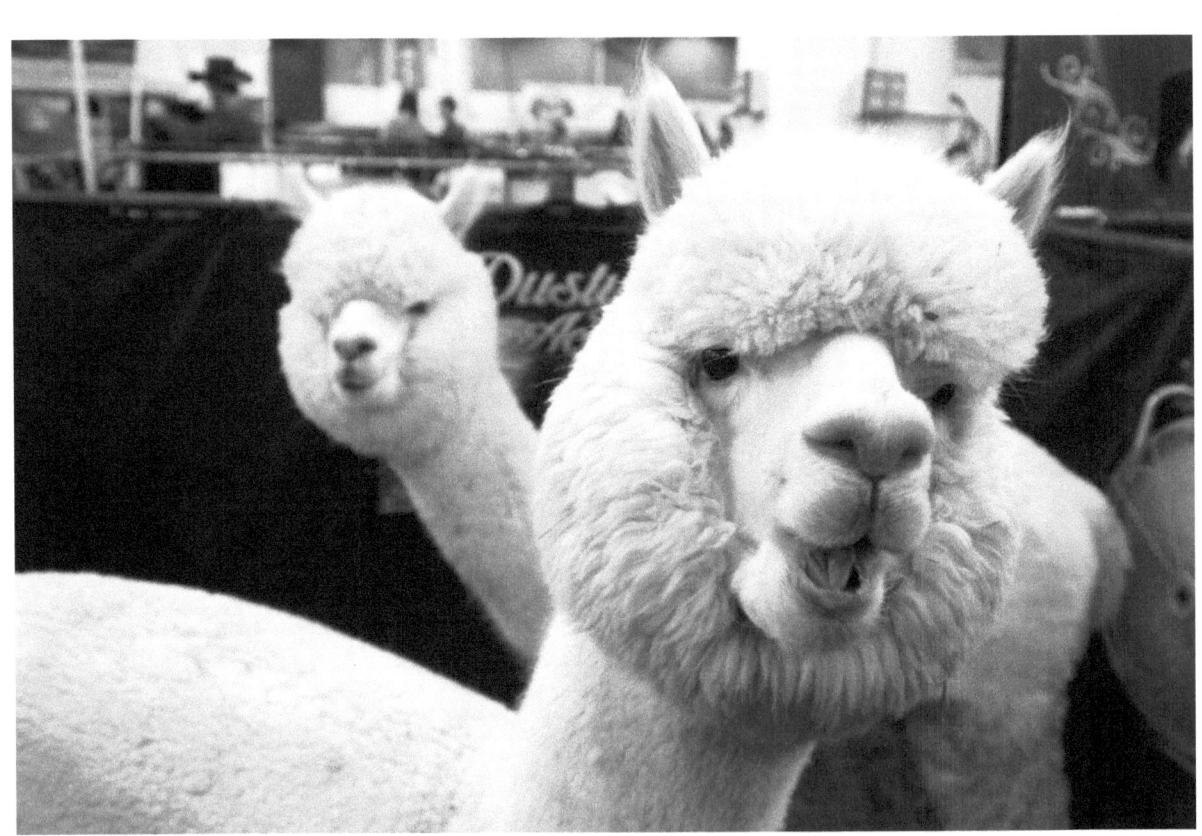

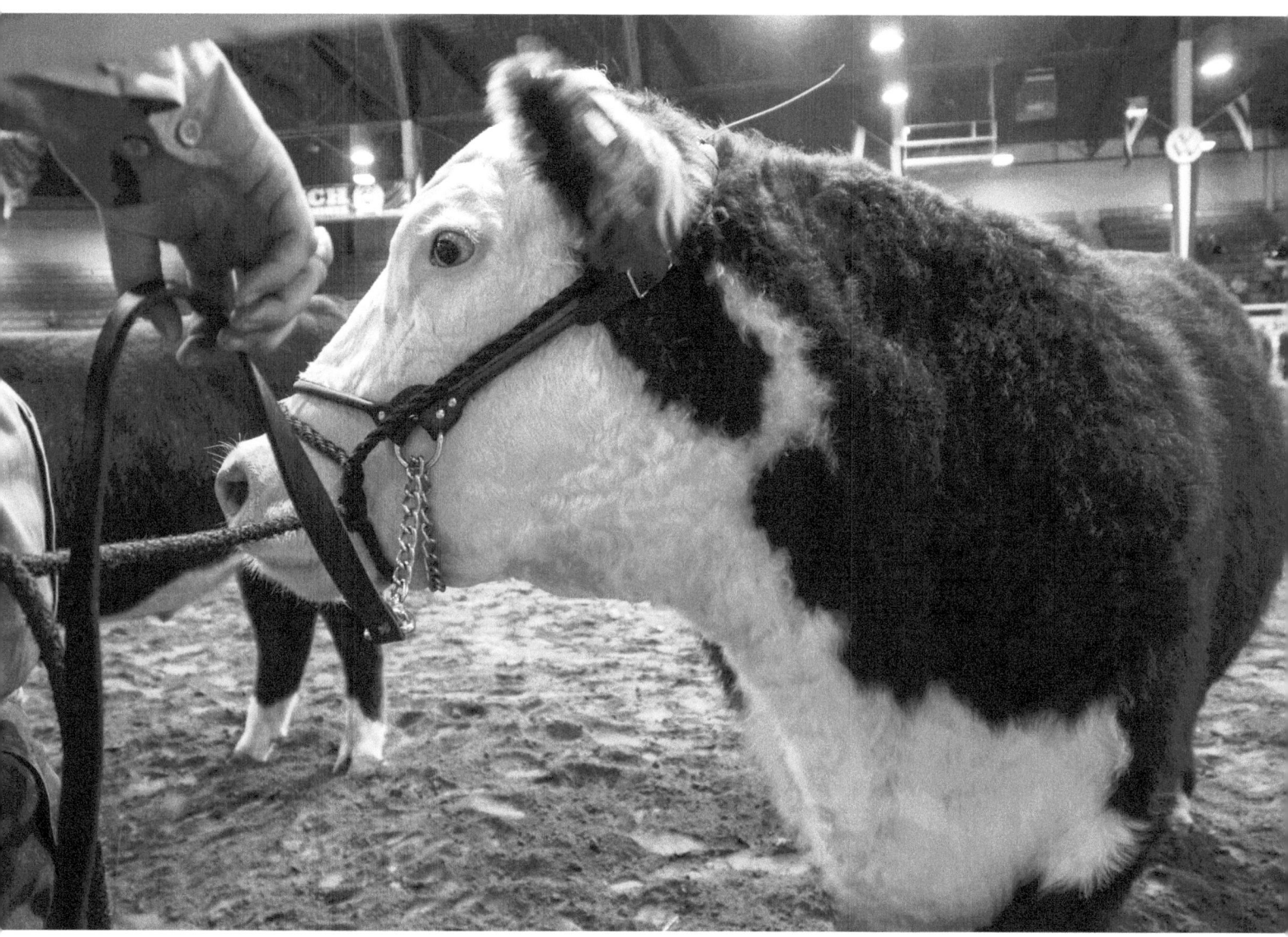

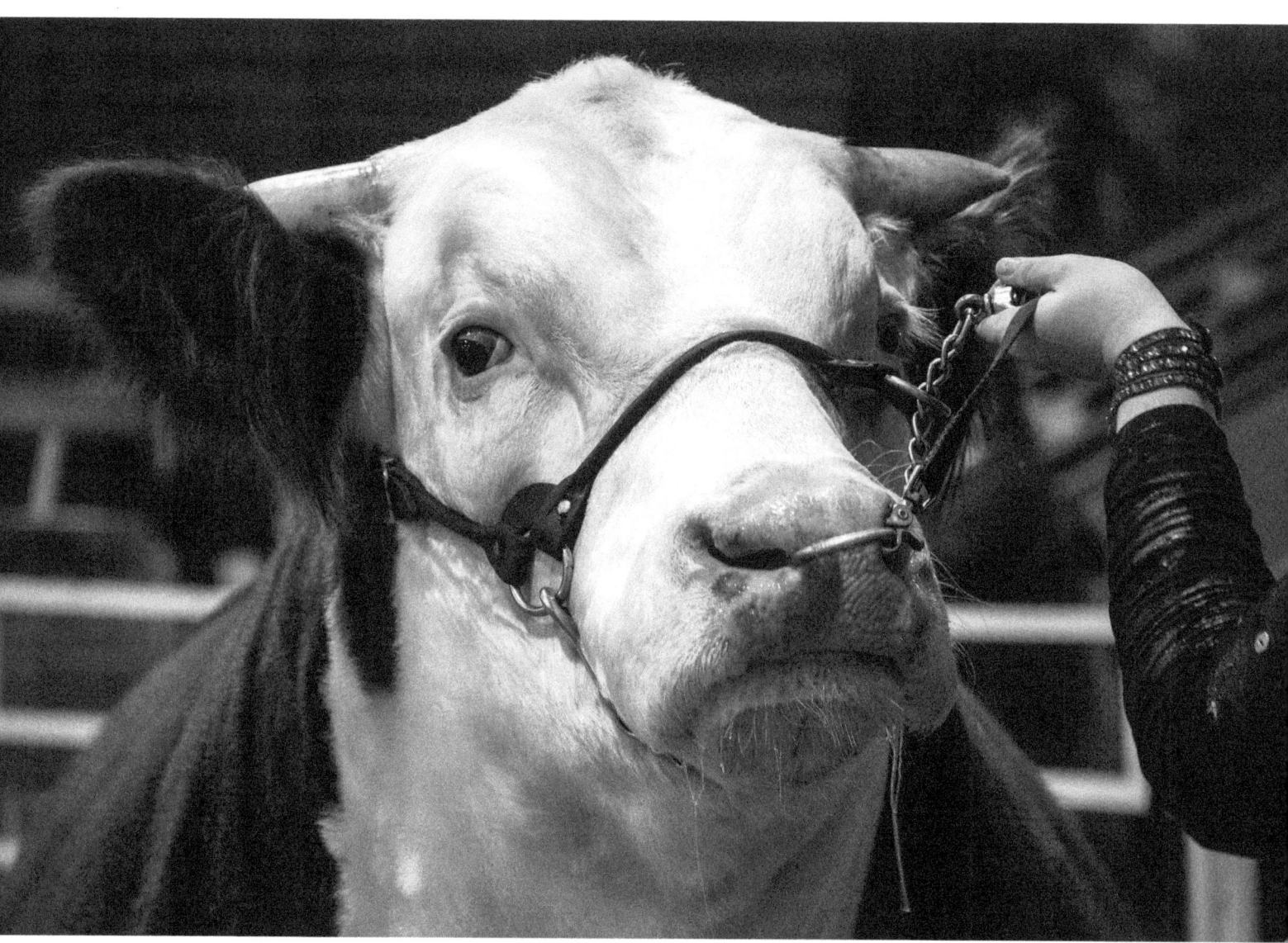

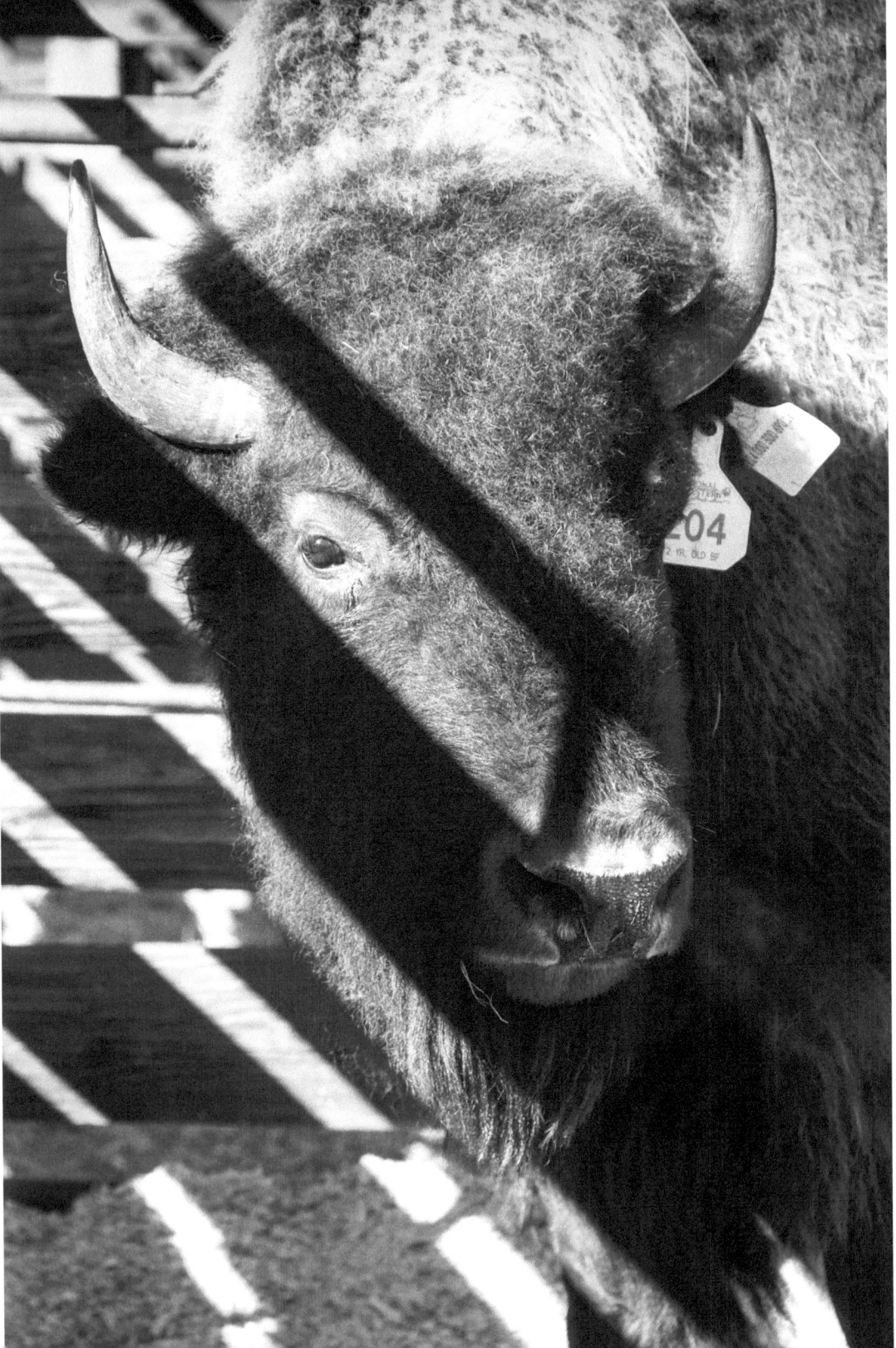

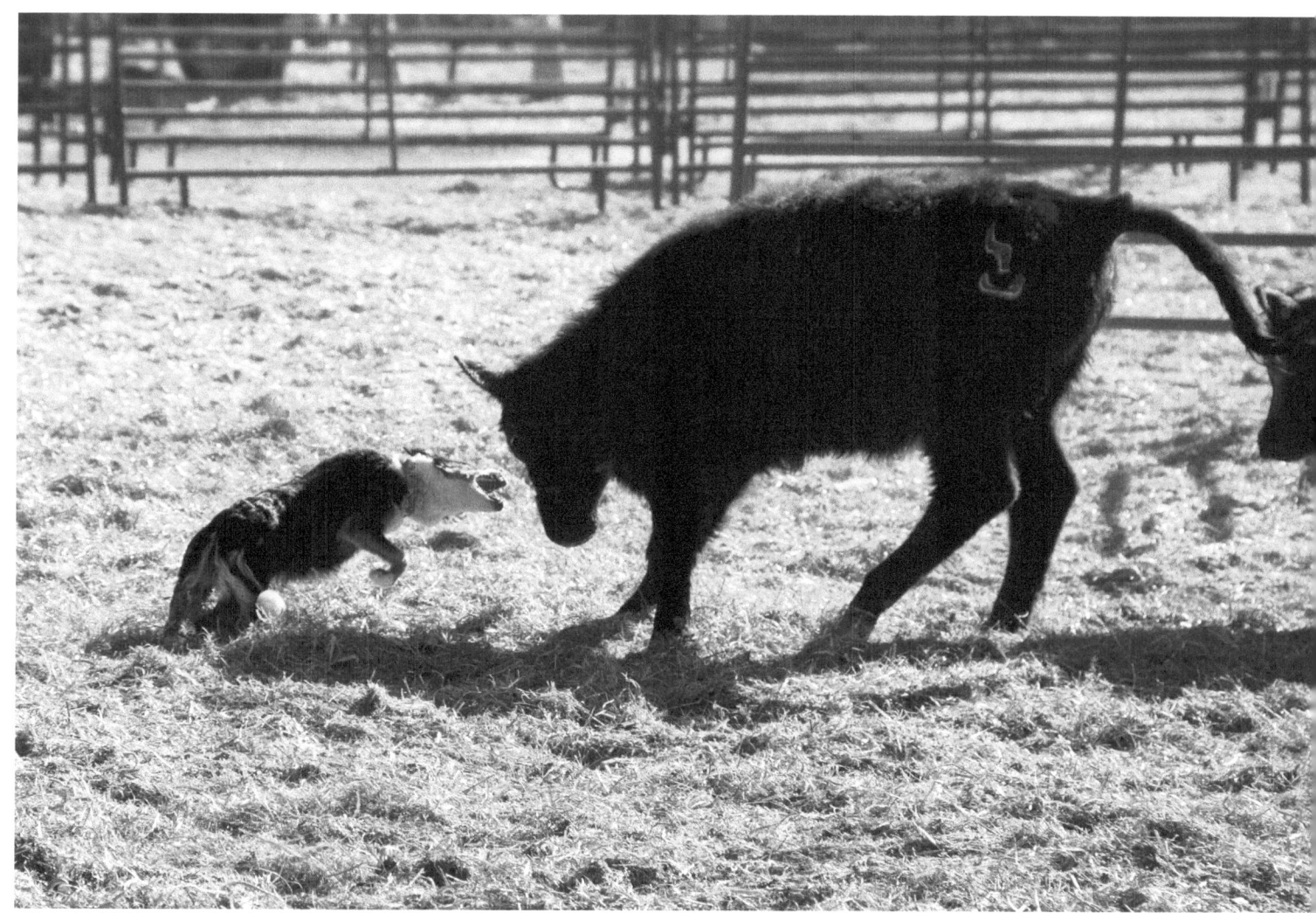

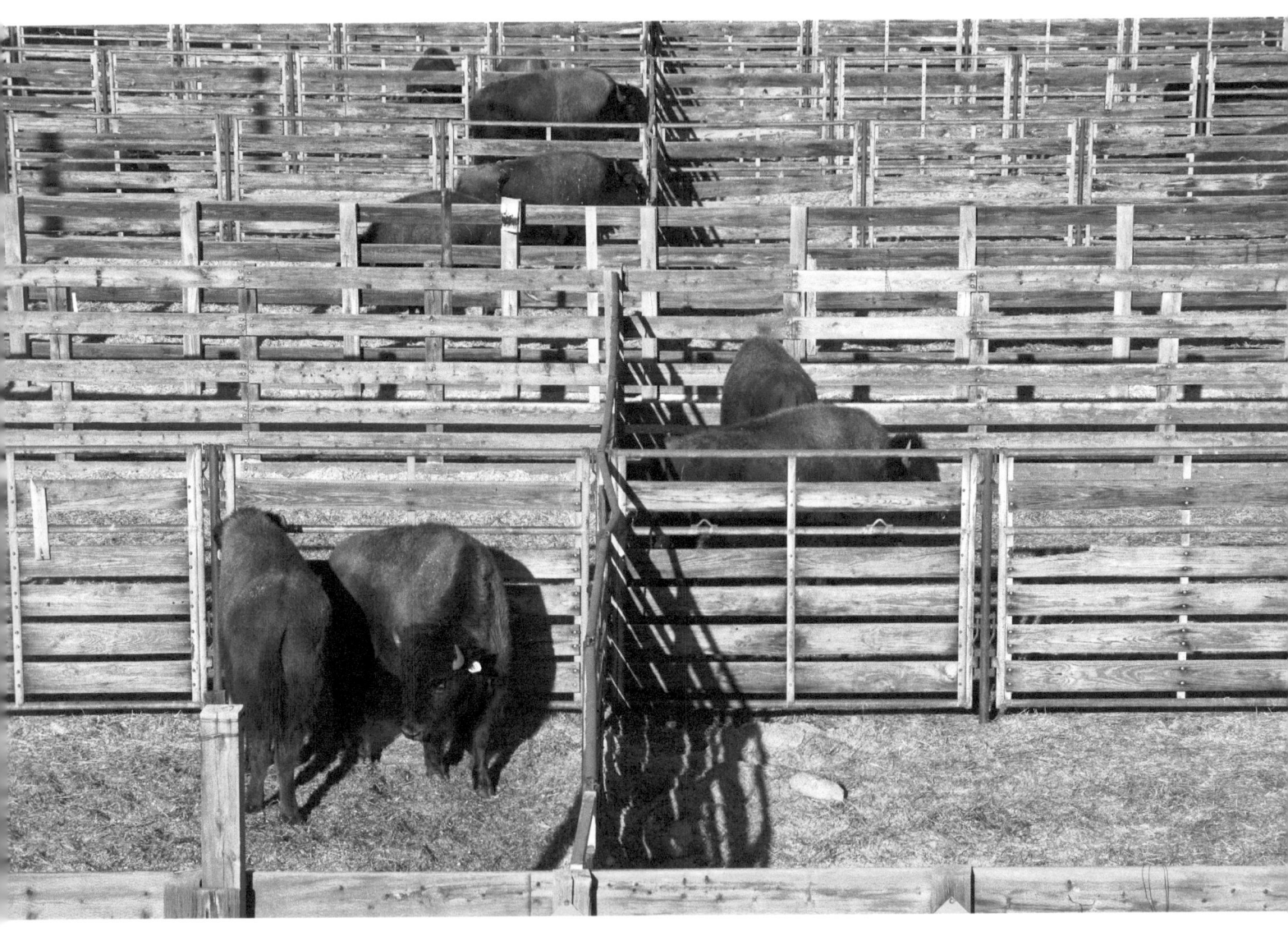

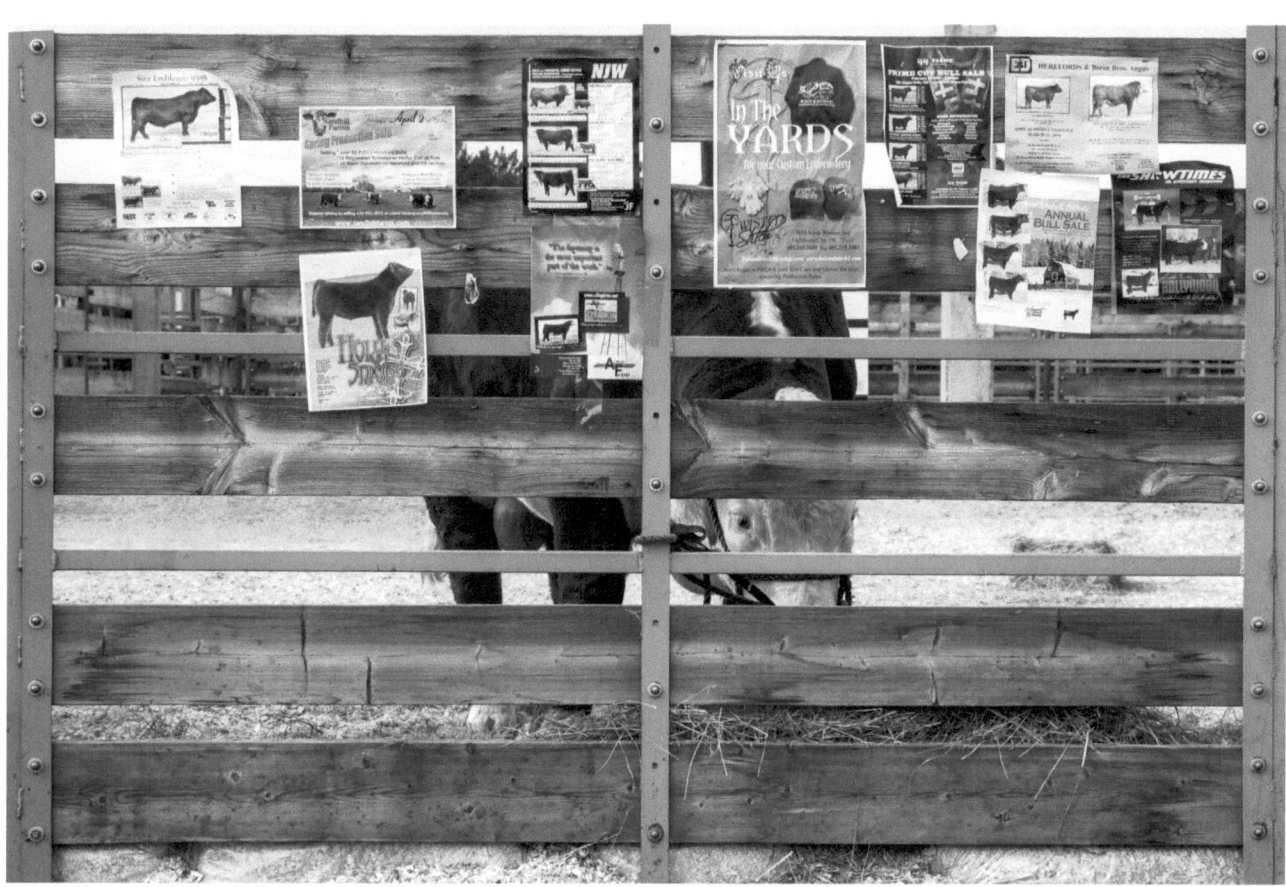

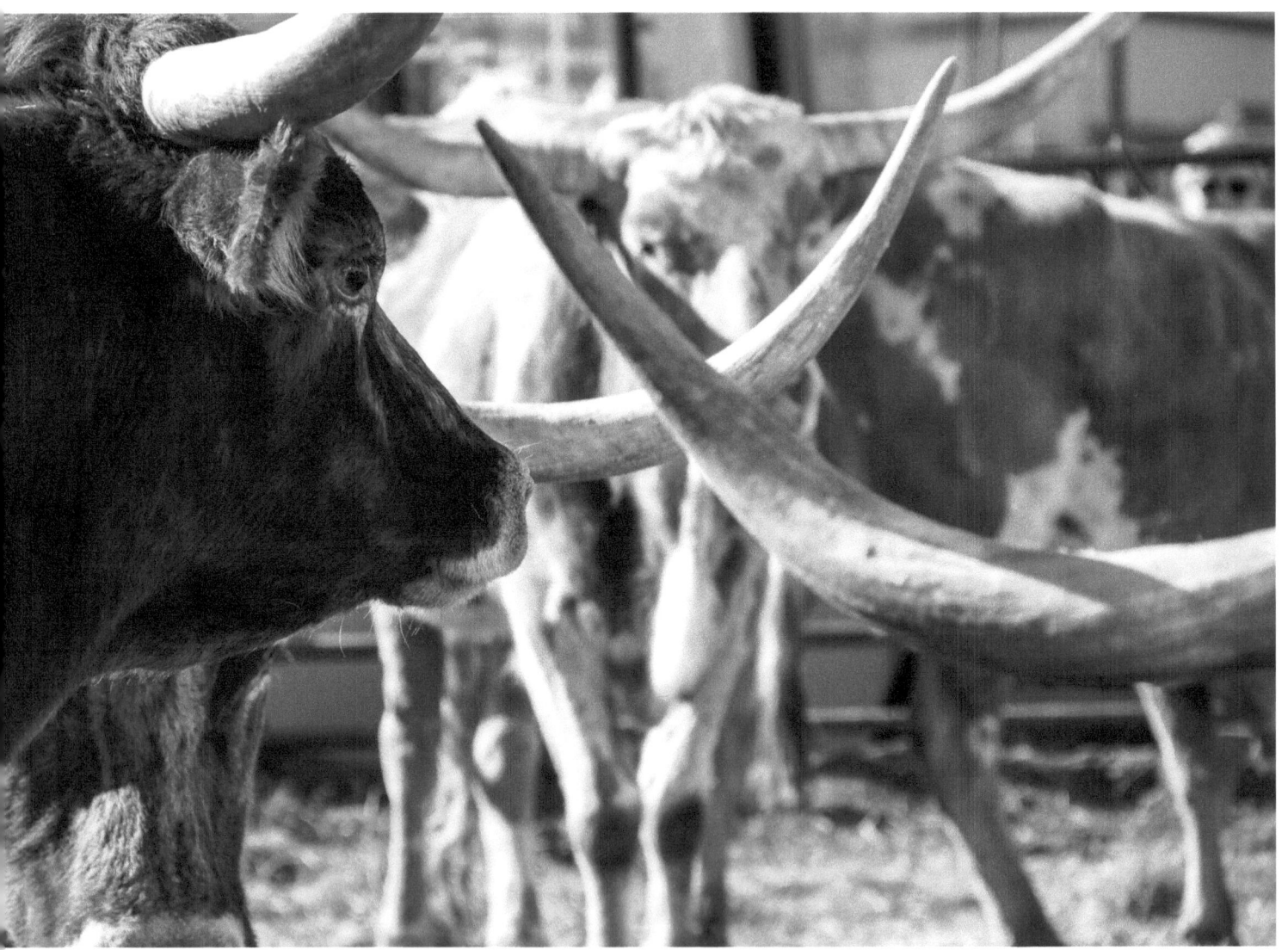

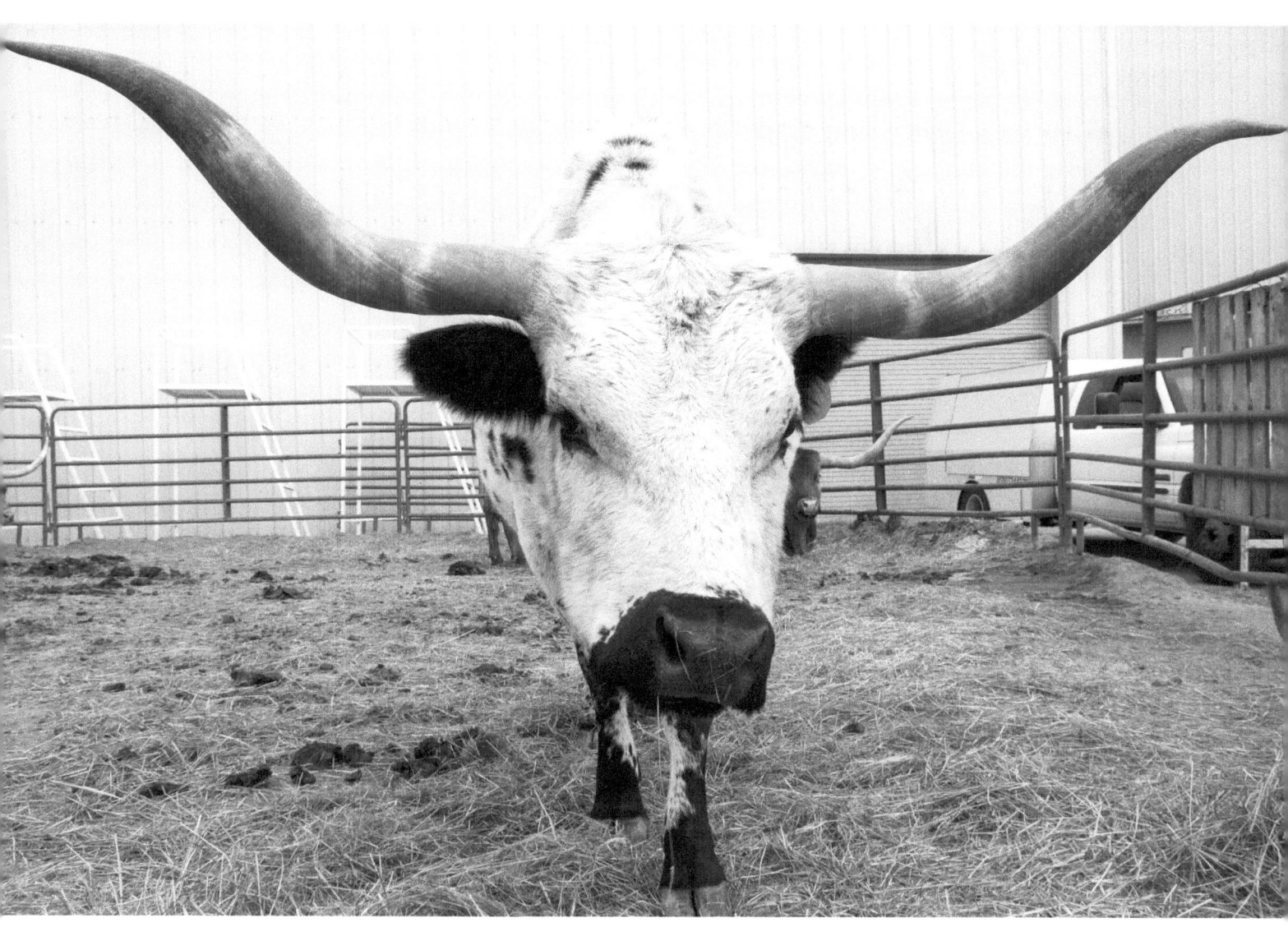

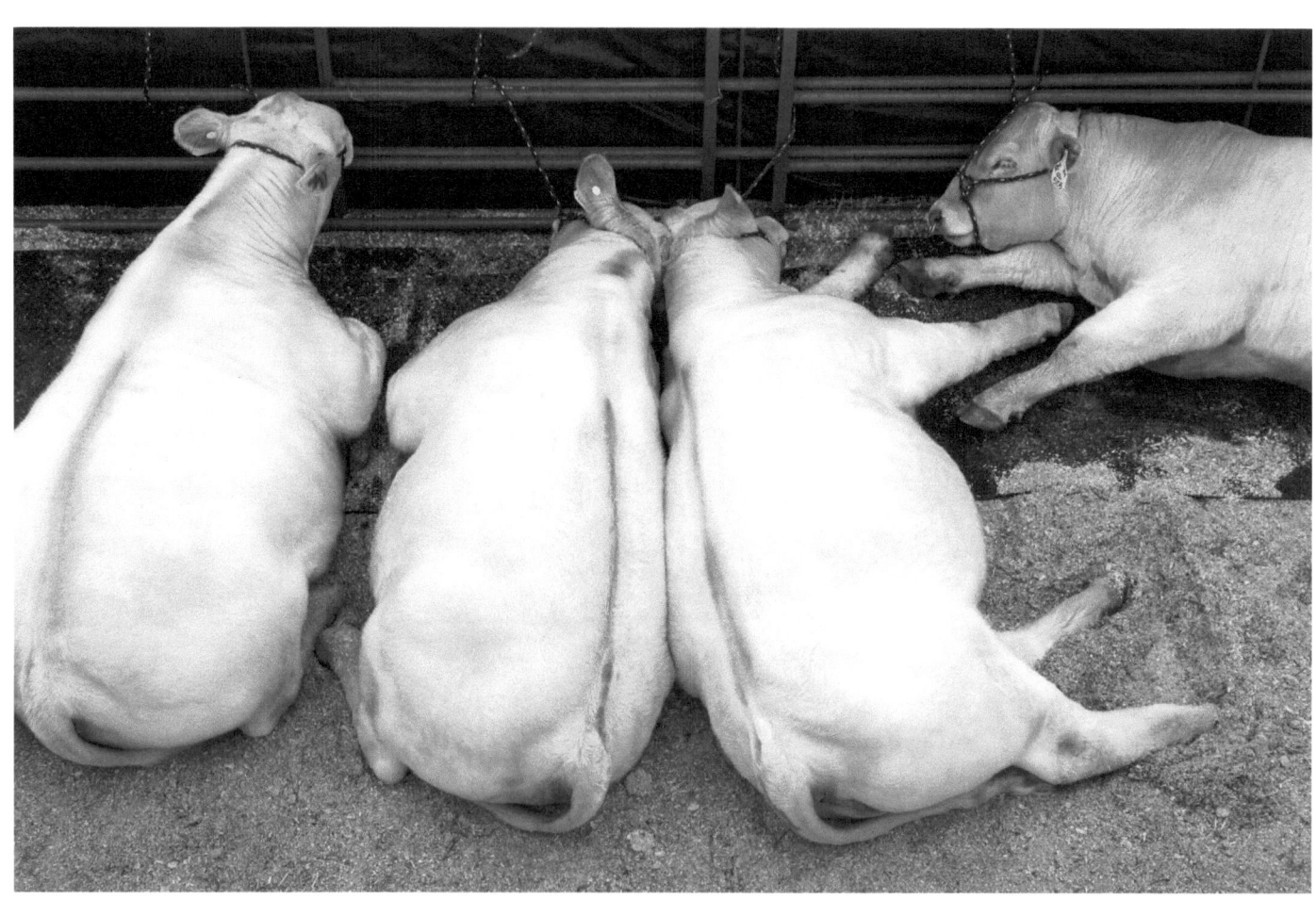

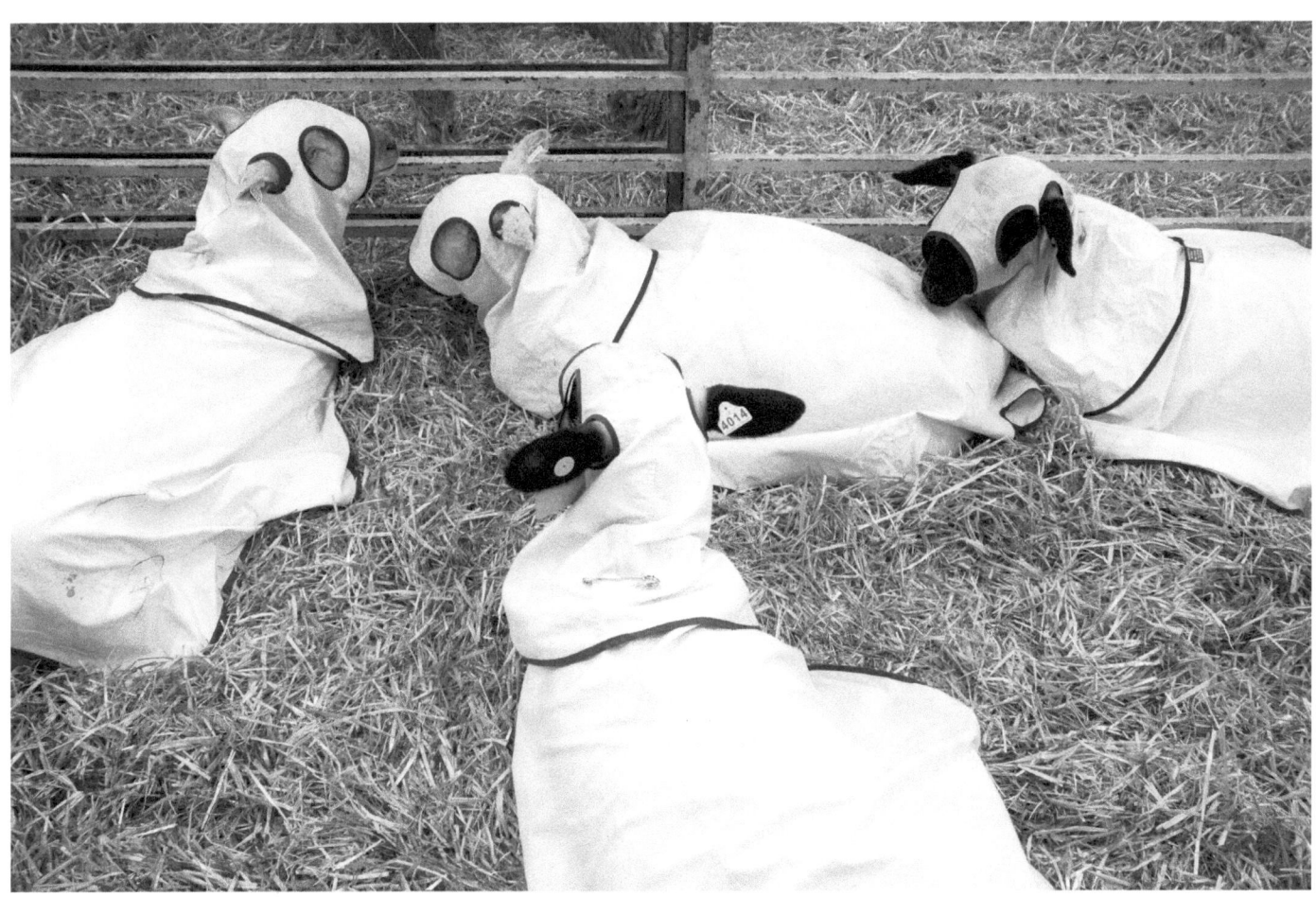

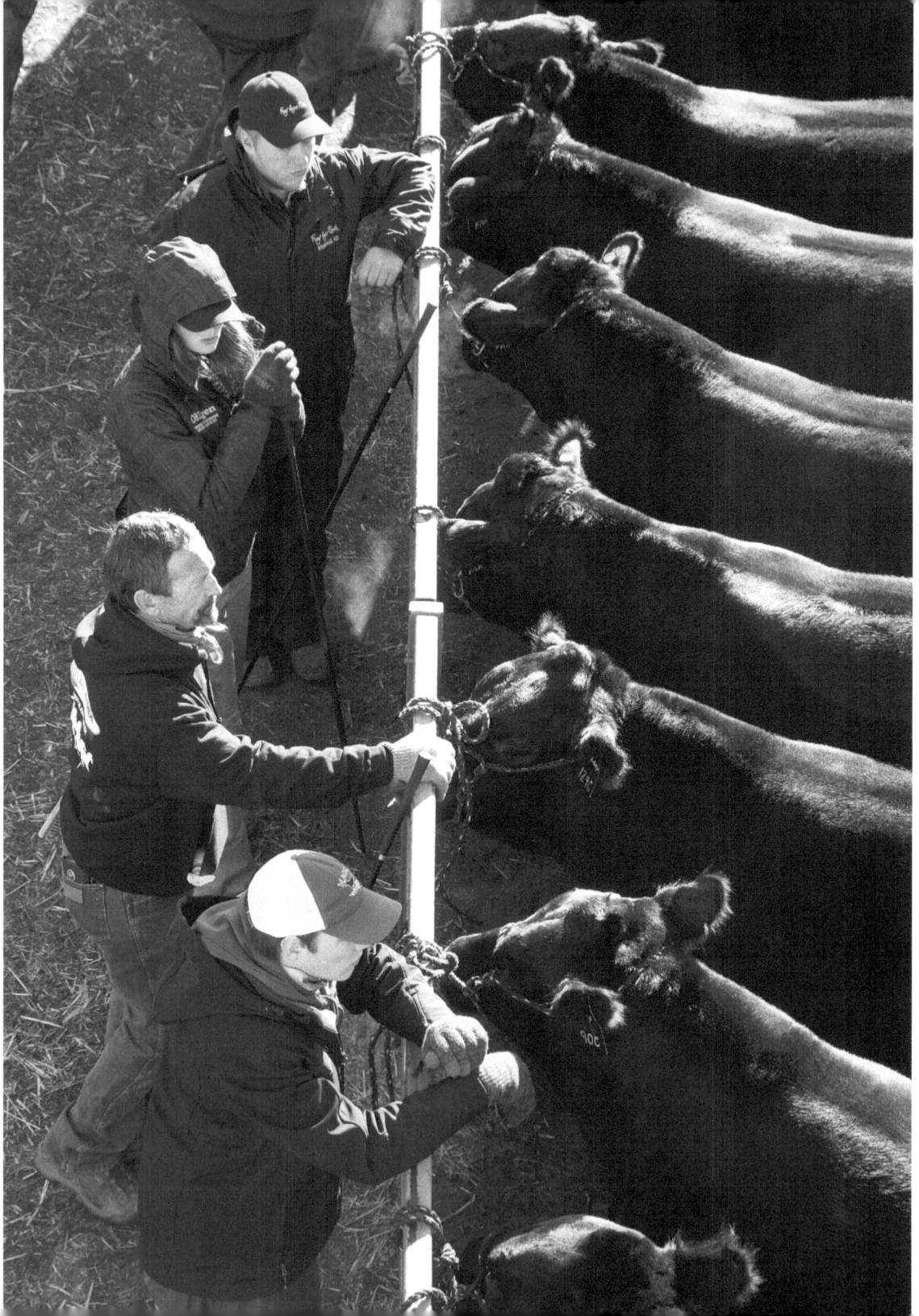

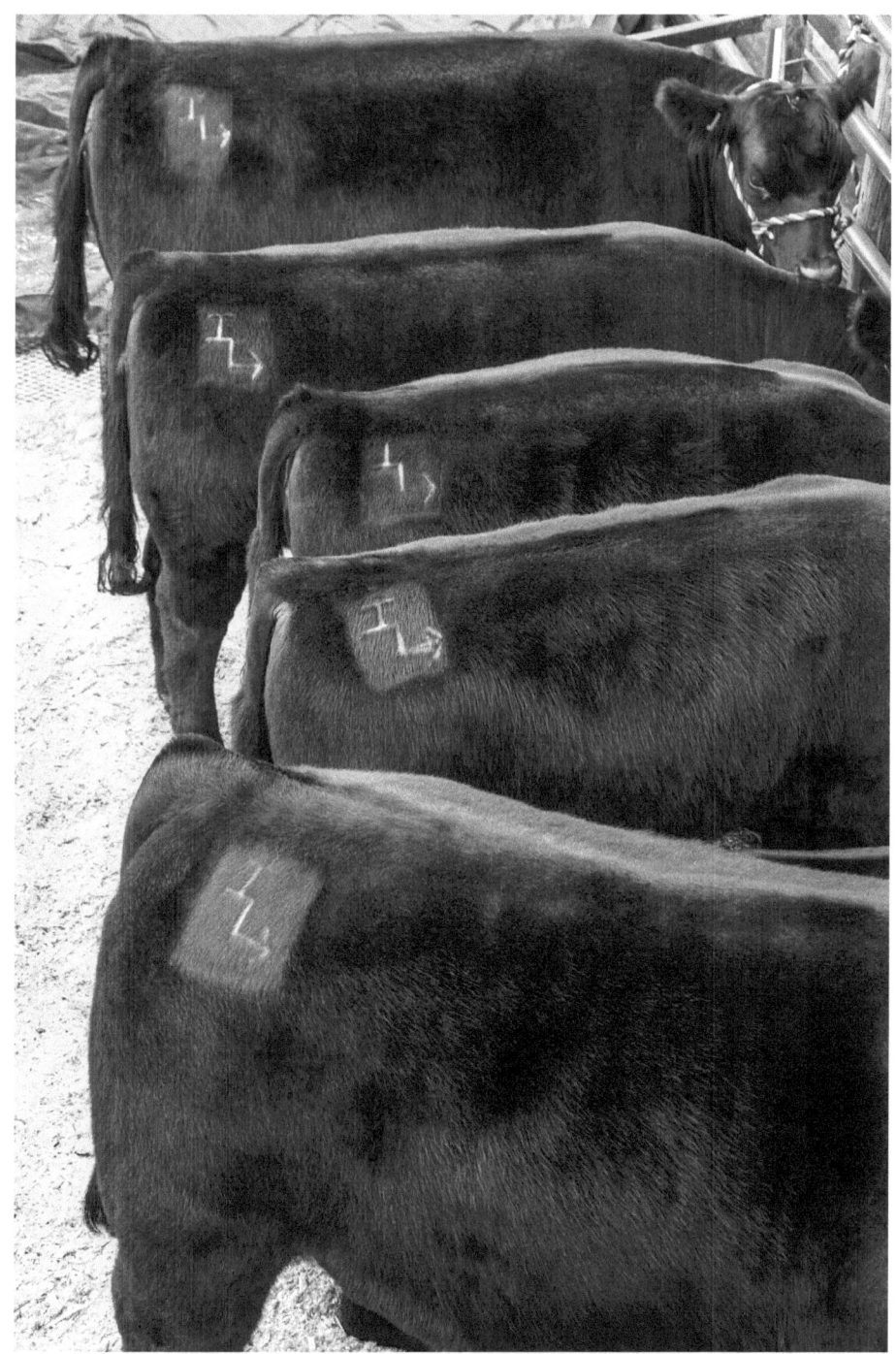

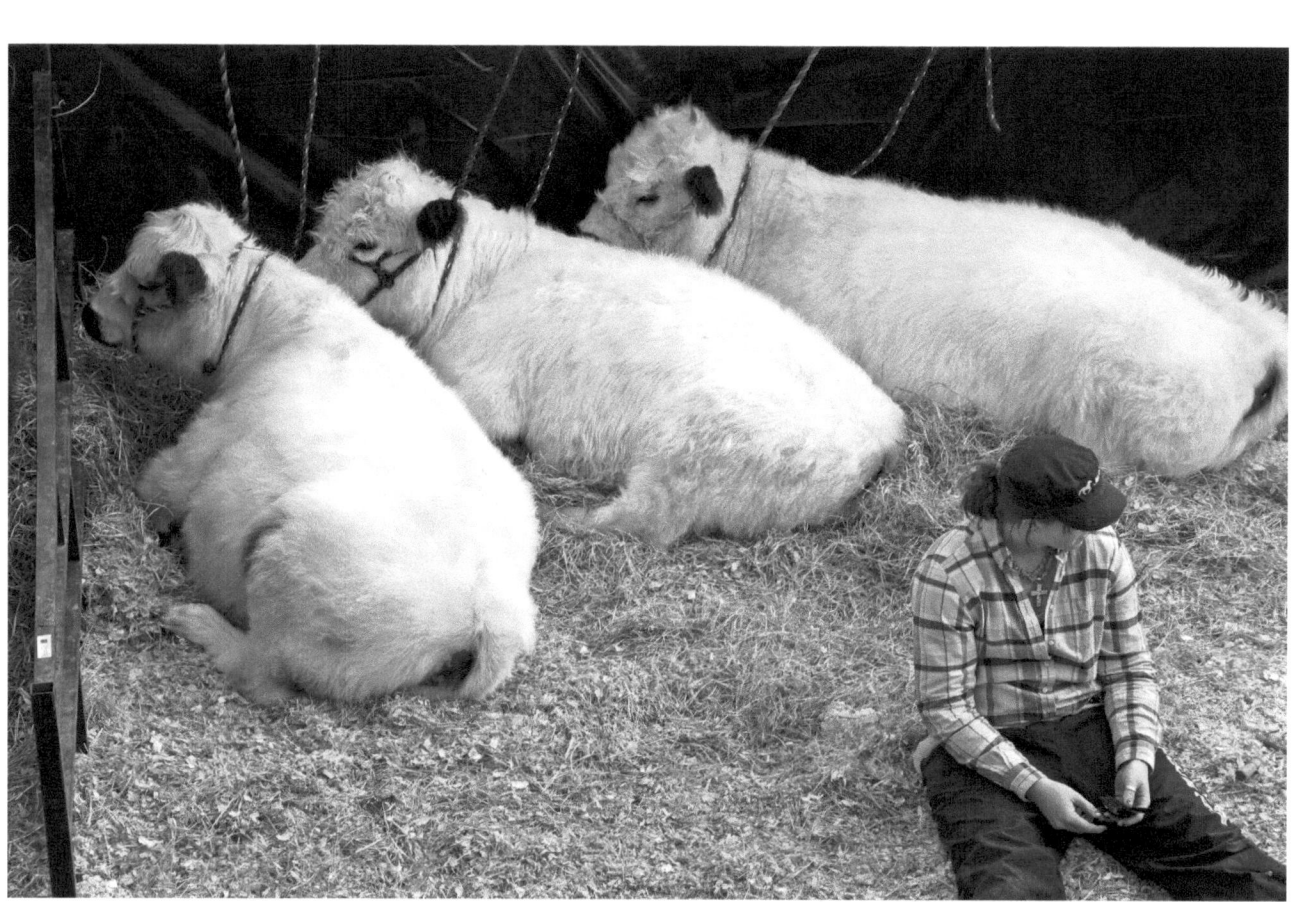

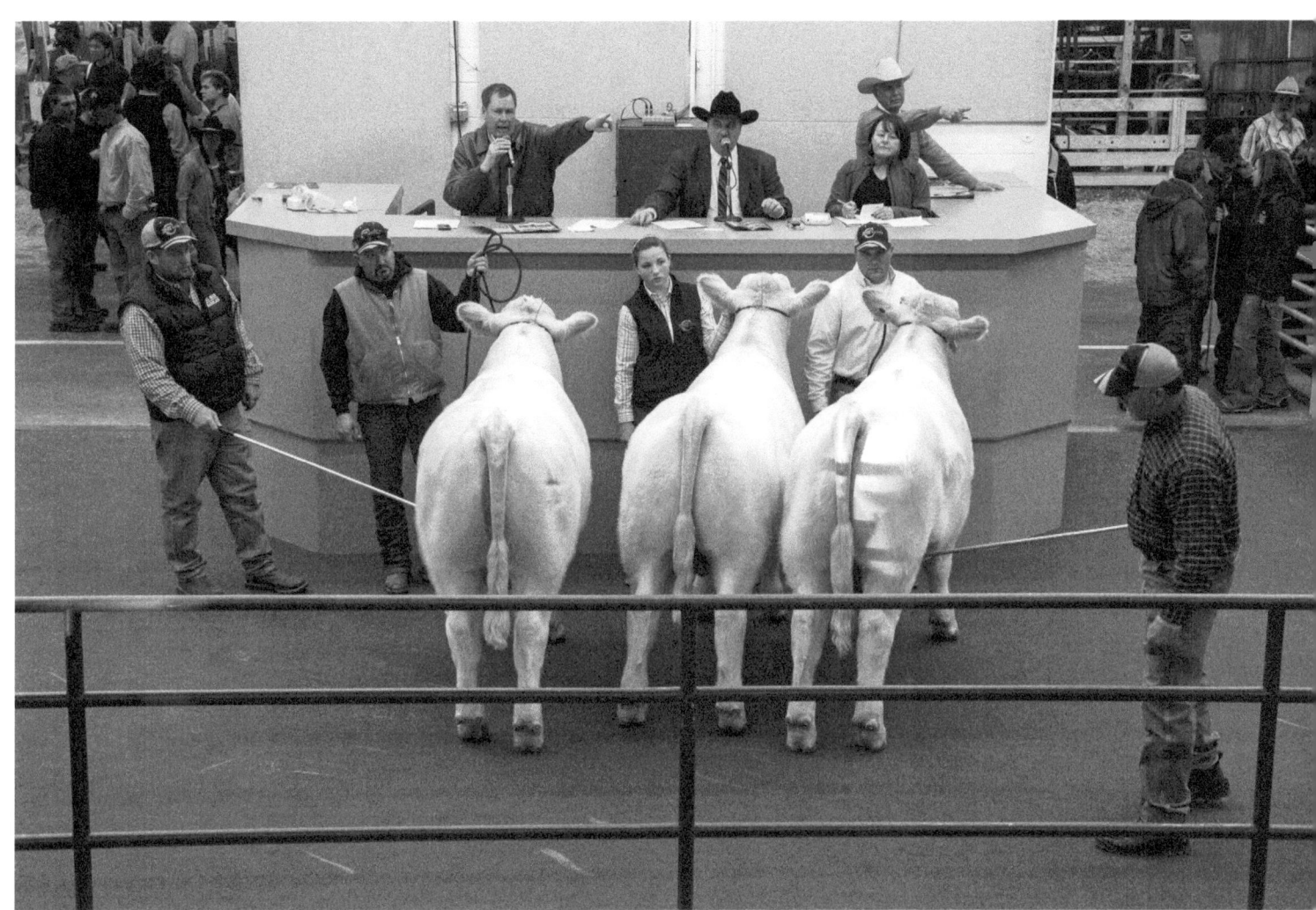

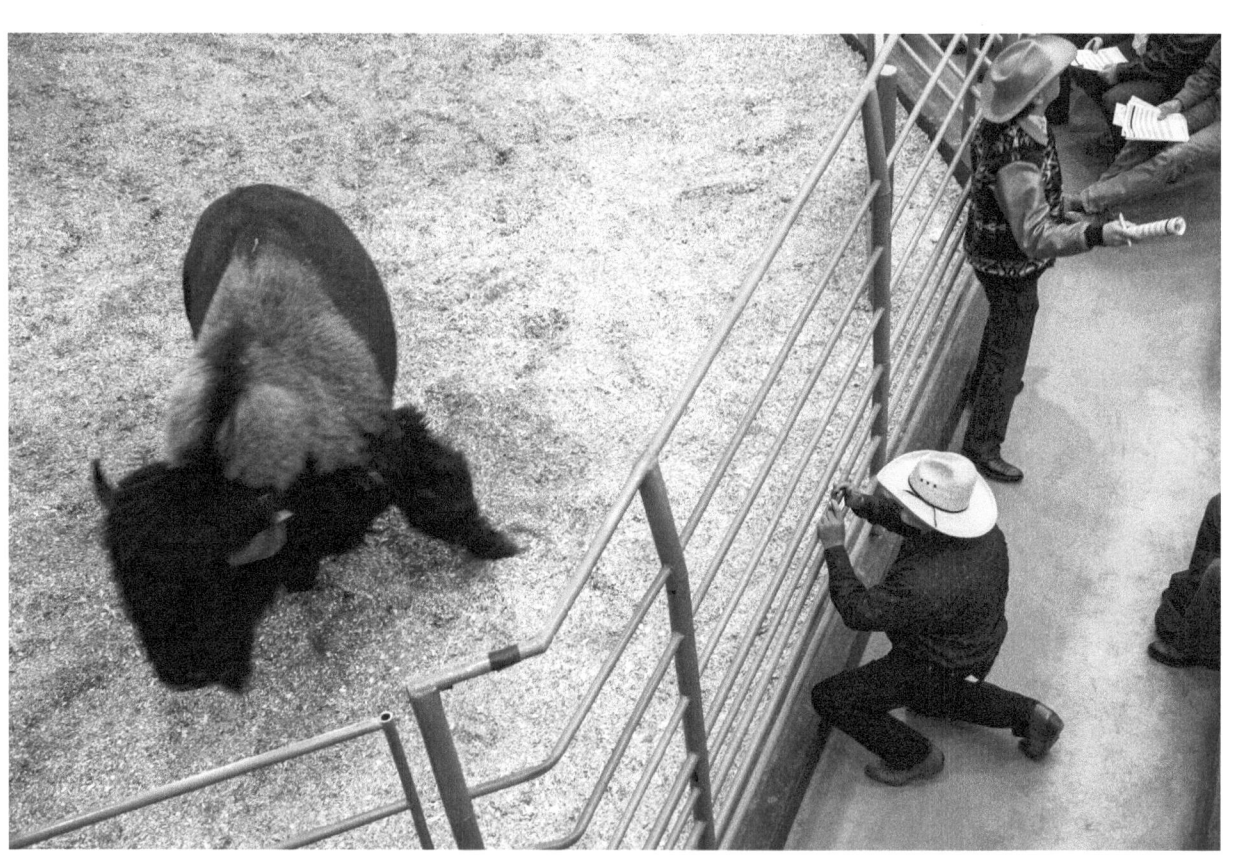

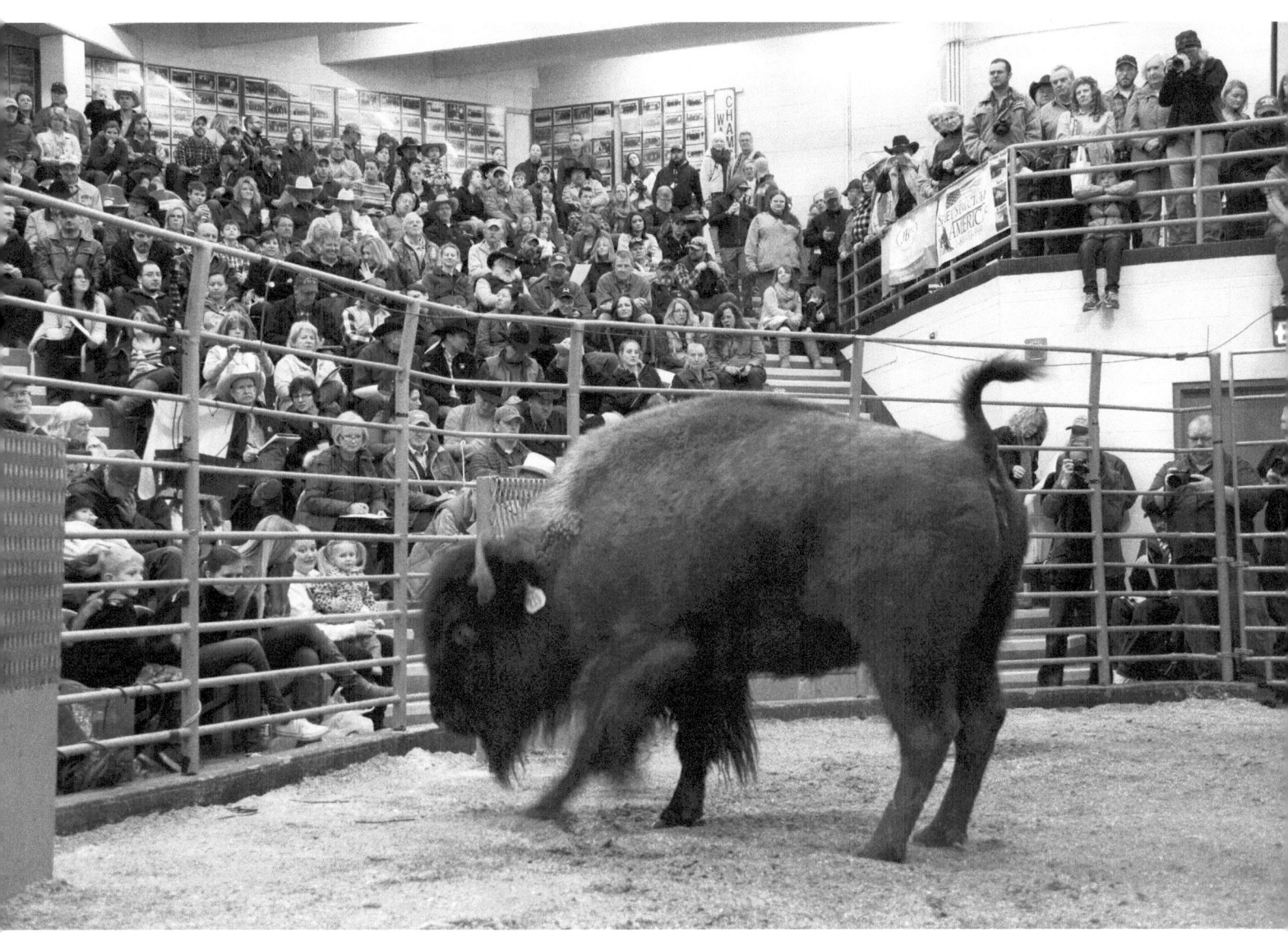

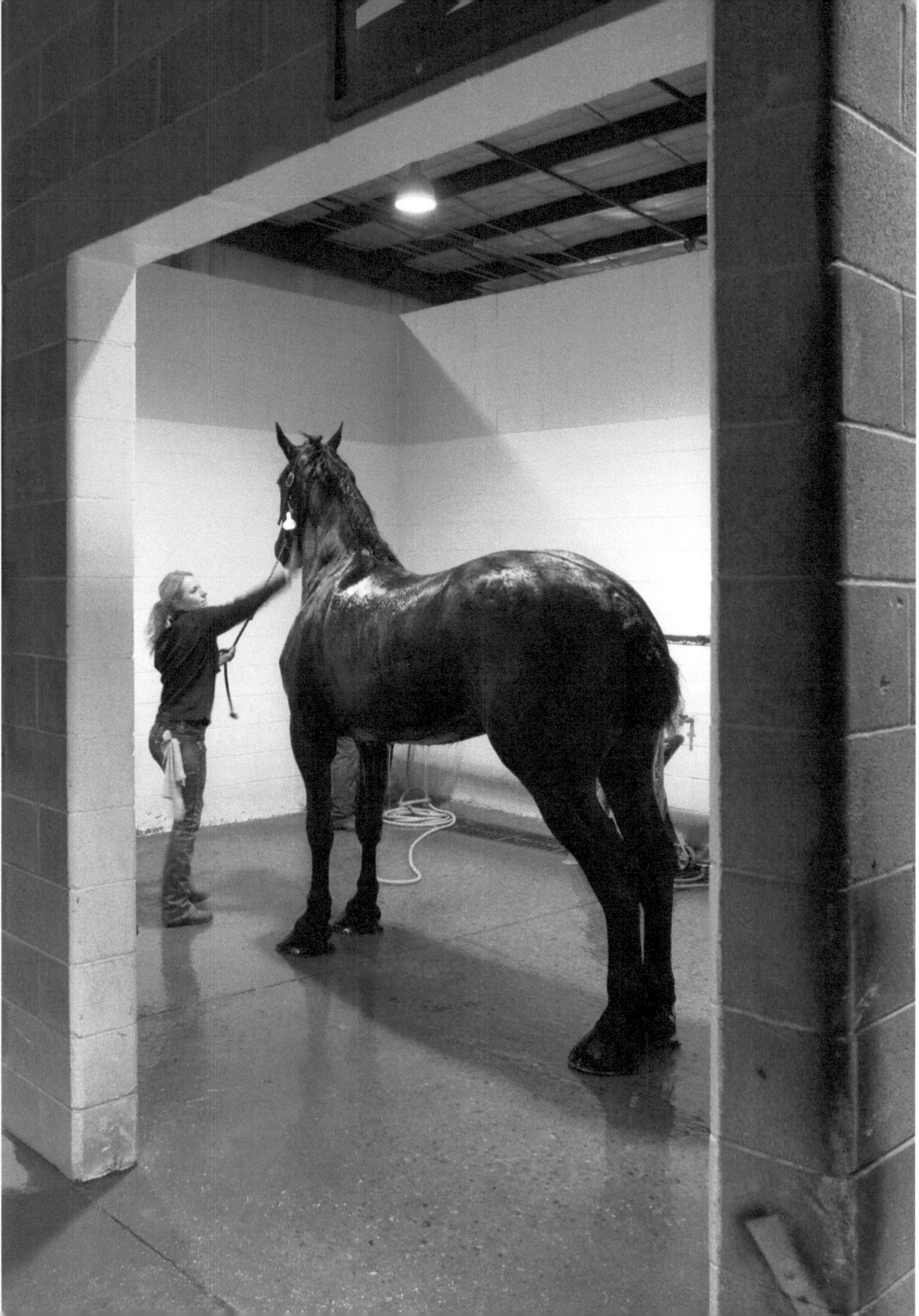

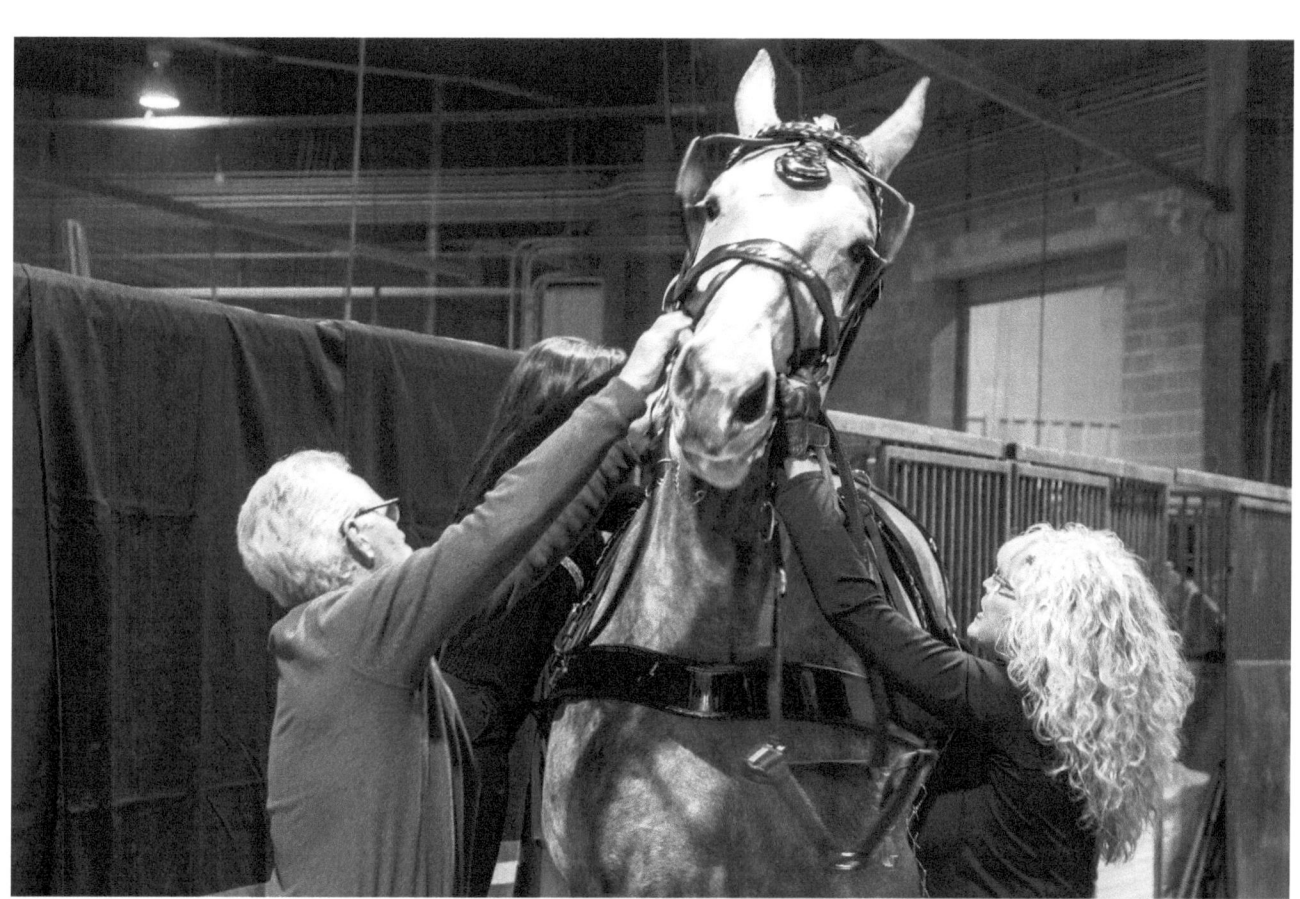

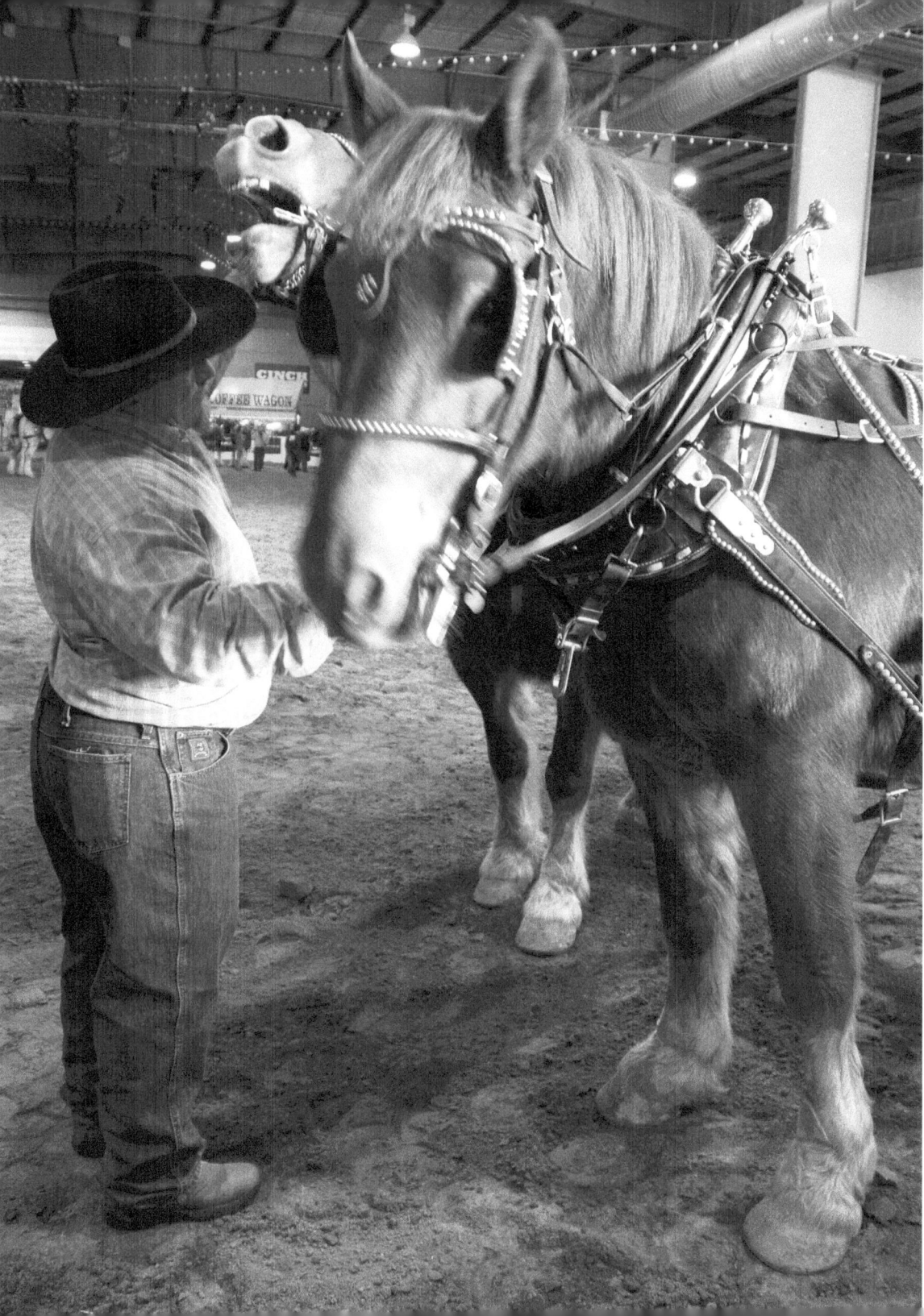

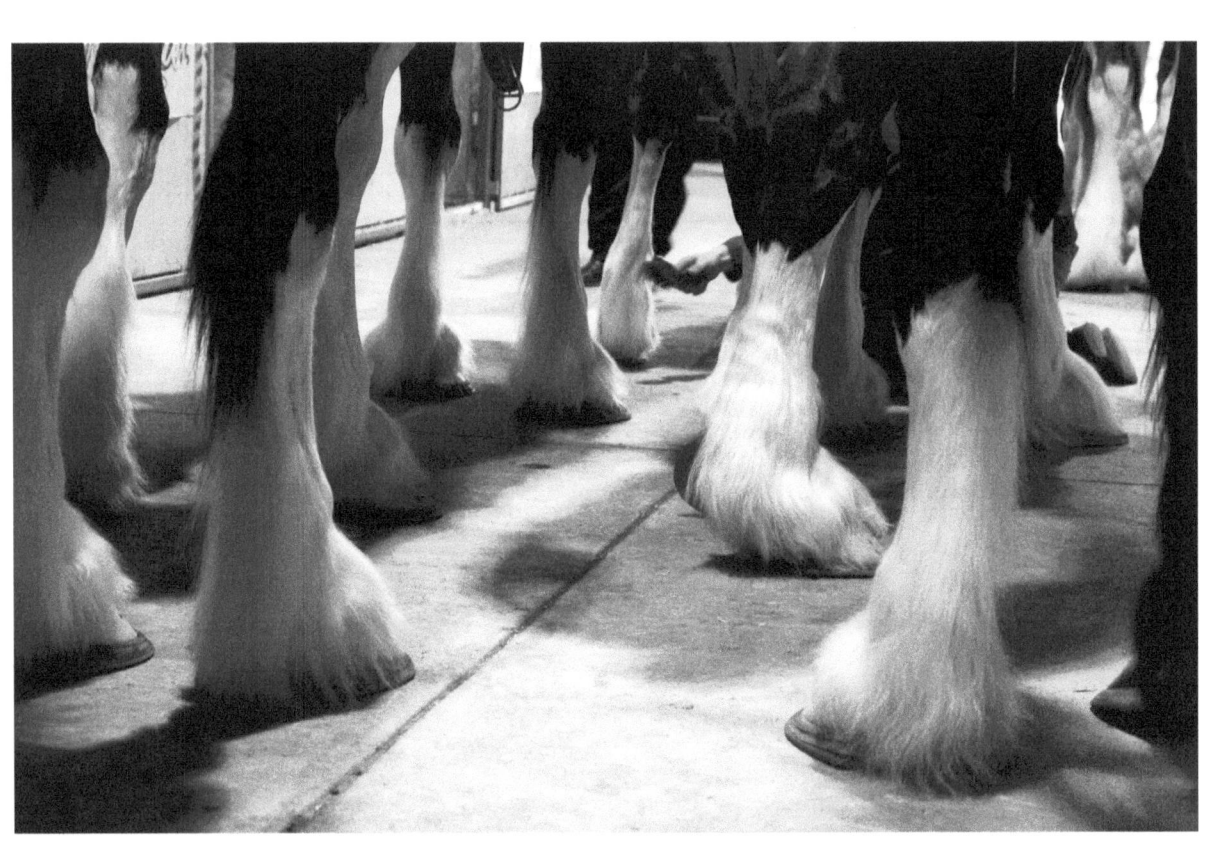

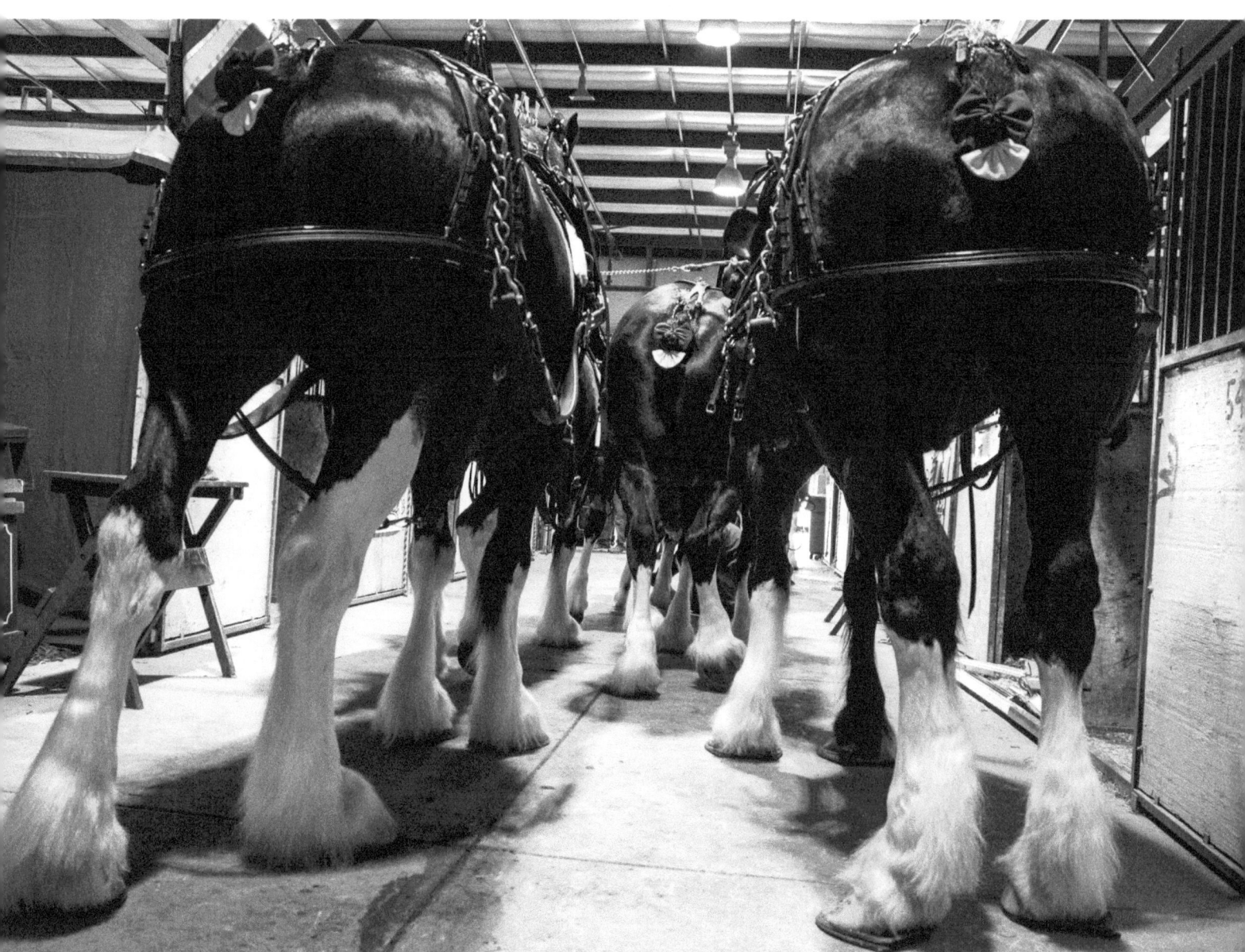

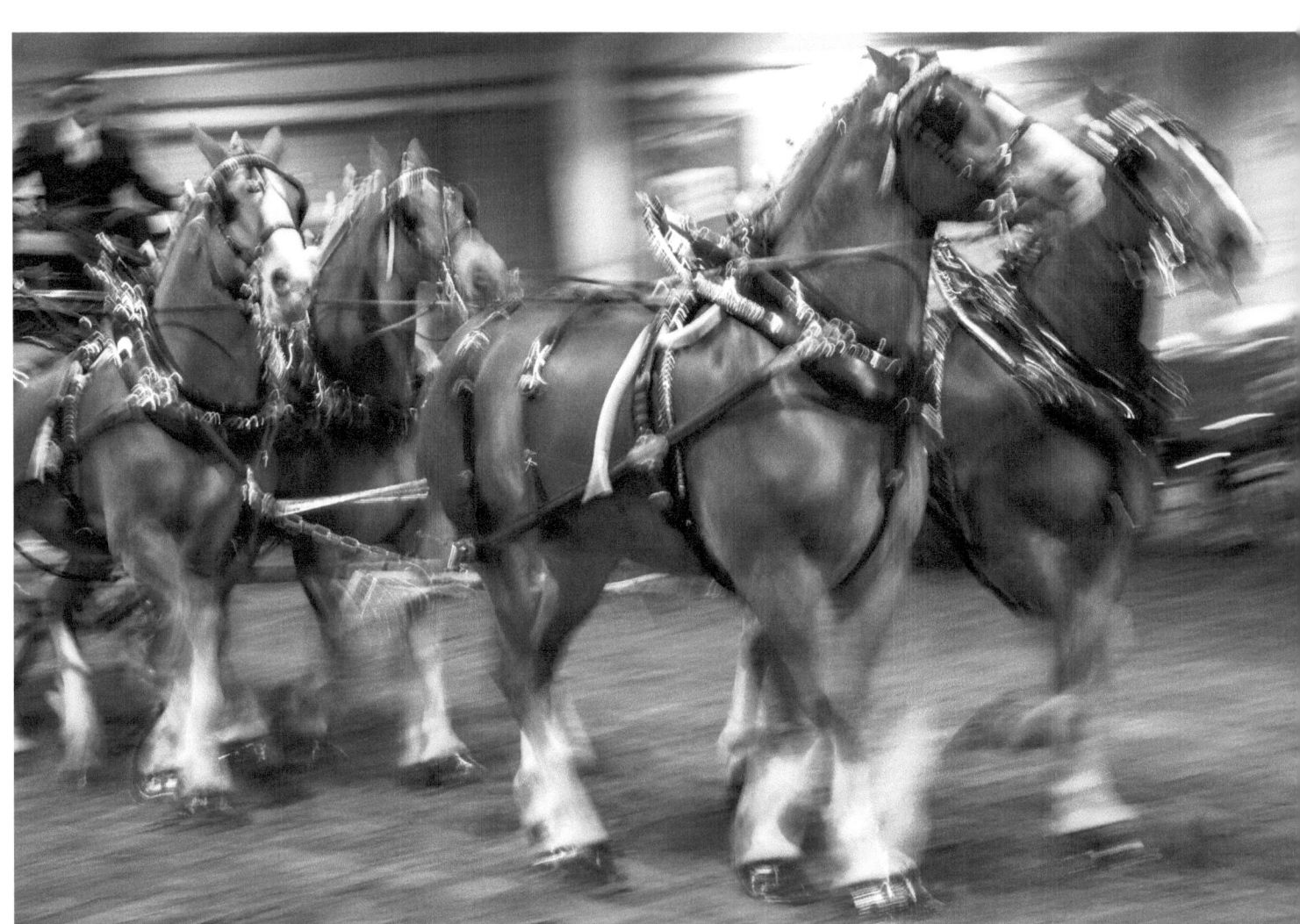

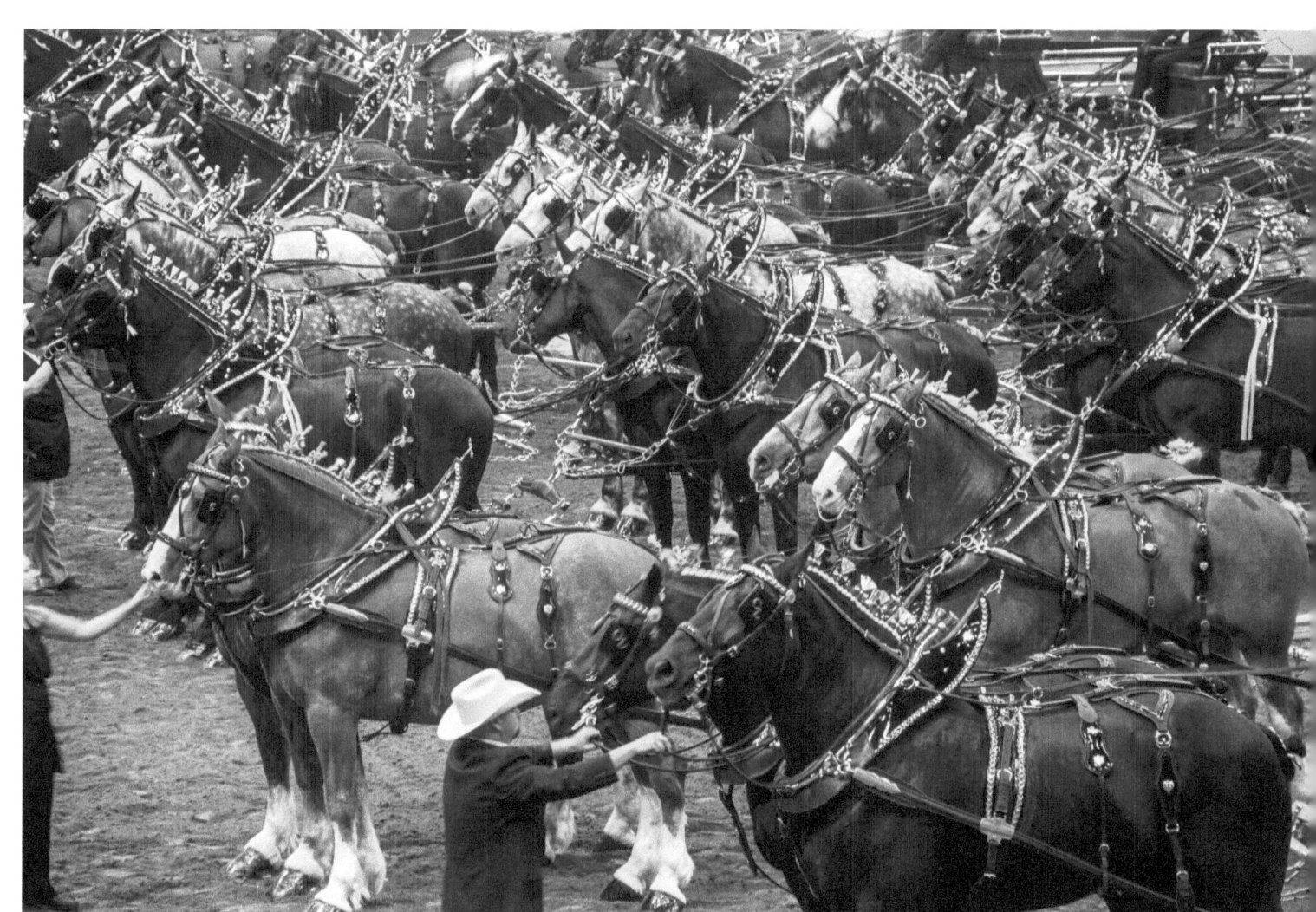

www.ingramcontent.com/pod-product-compliance
Lightning Source LLC
Chambersburg PA
CBHW050836180526
45159CB00004B/1928